MW01127280

Simple
Lean Six Sigma

*Global Organizational Lean Six Sigma Training for
Systematic Improvement – Driving Organizational
Excellence using Lean and Six Sigma*

Deisell Martinez, PhD

EDITION 2.1

Simple Lean Six Sigma
TABLE OF CONTENTS:

VOC
FMEA
Fish Boll

Pardad
ImR
control
Cause & EFF
Mectrics

Chapter 1:

Introduction

What is one of the largest risks an organization or individual faces? The risk of the unknown.

The unknown happens for a number of reasons, such as unplanned events. There are two types of unplanned events:
1. Those which are out of the realm of one's control and could not have been anticipated/prepared for.
2. Those that ARE within the realm of one's control and would have been projected for consistent outcomes regardless of 'who' or 'what', with timely planning and preparation.

What is the result of the unknown? Mistakes; which, in a company lead to customer complaint, products deemed unfit for use, increased costs and lost opportunities.

How can we plan and prepare for the unknown?
In most instances, we can use the past to try to determine what will happen in the future. As an example, if you have a co-worker and each time you are assigned to complete a project jointly, he or she does not come in, or return your calls. As a result, you always decide to work overtime and get the project done on your own. You would love to tell your boss, but your co-worker is an intimate friend. So, you just take care of the issue on your own.

With this in mind, if your boss requests a project and asks you to choose your team, you have three choices:
1. Use the past experience to determine that you will not have your old project partner again.
2. Choose your old project partner again so your friend does not get angry with you, but this time plan your schedule and do the entire project yourself.
3. Choose your old project partner, split the work and plan to review it on a predetermined date with your boss as a team. However, on the date of the presentation, your partner calls in sick and fails to send you his/her part of the project for you to present. As a result, you are not prepared and your boss is extremely disappointed.

At first sight, the last scenario seems to be an unexpected event that led to a bad outcome. However, if you look closely you will notice that this is a normal pattern of behavior for your partner and the outcome may have been different choice of partner.

Lack of decision making skills, as in the example above, lead to poor 'unexpected' outcomes, and happen normally within individuals' lives and organizations.

What is a process?

A process is a series of interrelated events/activities that lead to a final outcome. Most people do not think in terms of a process. Rather, individuals are preconditioned to believe that outcomes are the result of a series of events. This belief leads to helpless sentiment and behavior. Whereas, understanding that a process is a series of inter-related activities that can be realigned to change the outcome to a desirable one, leads to a sense of empowerment and drive to make a difference.

How can outcomes be altered, or enhanced, by plan and preparation?

Have you ever heard of *Process (Performance) Improvement (P²I)*? It is the act of <u>analyzing a process</u> (macro or micro) to determine how it can be done better, and proceed to make the necessary changes such that the next occurrence of the event has better outcomes.

There are two possible paths to follow when choosing to drive *(P²I)*:

- *Unstructured*; this is commonly followed. It is reflected when an organization mandates performance enhancement, but does not provide an organized method by which to enhance performance. In this case, the outcome relies on individual expertise of driving improvements. And, when people do not meet their performance, they are penalized.

- *Structured* performance enhancement is less common, but most effective. It requires top management to collectively decide how the organization will improve (i.e. what will be the focus, how will it be measured and who will be responsible). A standard form to drive the improvements is determined and tied to reports that gage the status of the initiative(s). If the initiative(s) is unsuccessful, the approach is revisited for further enhancement. In this case, the focus is always the 'system' the organization provides, and not the 'individual.' The individual is penalized only when resisting collaboration with the educational and growth structure of the organization; that is, when the respective person becomes a roadblock.

What is Lean, Six Sigma, and Simple P²I, and how does it help you plan and prepare?

Lean Six Sigma and Simple P²I are standard forms to drive improvements in a macro or micro process.

Lean provides a set of transitional industrial engineering tools that identify valuable and invaluable activities within events and/or series of events. The analysis pinpoints specific improvements by eliminating those events or activities that incur costs, but are not valuable to the desired results.

Six Sigma is both a State of Performance and a Methodology.

It is a state of performance because, statistically, it refers to an expected number of acceptable and unacceptable results due to the nature of the data distribution. We will develop this concept in detail later in this book.

Six Sigma is also a tested and commonly known method with comprehensive data-driven tools supported by statistical analysis that reduce the risk of the unknown.

Lean and Six Sigma combined minimize costs and unpredictable, but potentially negative, outcomes.

One of the drawbacks of Lean and Six Sigma is the level of complexity; as, it assumes an advanced fundamental understanding of processes and improvement tools/methods.

However, what if everyone thought and acted as an engineer and focused on patterns of events? Everyone would be focused on outcome efficiency and consistency.

Simple P²I^{TM} is a straightforward framework that uses a combination of key Lean and Six Sigma tools to drive quick and valuable improvements regardless of individuals' underlying training. This method is proprietary to DEIVIN, and is often used to reduce the P²I knowledge gap between management, professional employment and frontline workers such that all have the necessary fundamental knowledge and training to cohesively drive improvements and cultural transformation that enhance outcomes and sustainability – think and act like engineers.

This book explains Six Sigma as a State of Performance, highlights the fundamentals of P²I, introduces a realm of P²I methodologies and tools, and delineates the how to execute Lean Six Sigma.

Chapter 2:

Fundamentals of Process (Performance) Improvement P^{2}I

Change is most common under two environments:
1. *Crisis* due to extenuating circumstances, which leads the organization to minimize costs and/or maximize profits.
2. *Strategic Initiative* to change the organizational structure and/or culture.

In either of the above scenarios, leaders mandate change or seek to cohesively coordinate all resources in achieving their goal.

An argument can be made in the defense or criticism of a selected strategy. It is, however, important to analyze and understand the fundamental components that lead to success:

1. *Organizational Structure*
   Organizations with functional management structure are, mostly, partitioned into three tiers:

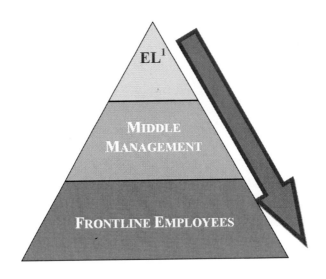

Figure1

2. *Core Drivers to Organizational Breakdown*

Simple Lean Six Sigma, Page 14 of 186

There are three core drivers to organizational breakdown:

- Leadership – the ability to analyze existing organizational and industry conditions in order to set a strategic plan by which to maximize profits and market share, while enhancing employee motivation and passion for their jobs as well as the organization.
- Teamwork – the ability to work together with clear communication and focus on identifying core issues as well as making sound data-driven recommendations and execution.
- Communication – the development and maintenance of a clear governance pathway with simple and clear measurable metrics that communicate successes and failures, risks and roadblocks.

3. *Vision, Mission, Strategy and Execution*

Focus is critical to organizational success. In doing this, organizations should set a vision, determine its mission, define strategic goals and develop an execution plan.

- *Vision.* A vision is a plan for the future of the organization. In the next 5, 10, 20 years, where does the organization want to be in comparison to today.
- *Mission.* A mission is the direction the organization chooses to take in order to achieve the vision.
- *Strategic Goals.* The specific milestones the organization need to achieve the mission.
- *Execution Plan.* A roadmap delineating *how* the organization will achieve its strategic goals. The roadmap should identify specific projects that will collectively serve to achieve the strategic goals. The projects should have clear deliverables that are easily measureable and have outlined metrics.

- Goals, within a strategic plan or project, need to be SMART: Specific, Measurable, Assignable, Realistic and Time related.

4. Core Skills

- No goal or path is unrealistic if the passion, drive and skills are present. There are two things that are critical to execution at any level:
    1. Will; the *want* to do whatever is set forth.
    2. Know-How, the notion or specific knowledge necessary to accomplish the set goals.

For the most part, employees want to perform well, get recognized and be given the opportunity to excel in their environment. The breakdown in non-performance as related to *will* and *know-how* is vague unless the organization trains its employees in a method(s) or set of tools for uniform use in driving performance improvement and enhancing the bottom-line.

**The above assumes organizations offer necessary resources, and support to resistance/roadblock in achieving goals. **

- Tiers of employment in organizations vary depending on level and nature of the organization's core business. For the most part, the education level in executive leadership and middle management is higher than that of the frontline workforce. However, it is the frontline workforce that develops products, and/or handles service calls/visits that directly impact the customer; and, therefore, quality. As such, it is important that the method(s) and/or tools selected address higher and lower education levels of the organization such that the entire workforce optimizes the communication stream to enhance performance.

The basics

As mentioned earlier, P^2I is the act of analyzing events to identify how they can be improved; and, proceed to make changes such that the next occurrence of the event has better outcomes.

Before jumping into this, let's clearly define a project. Traditional project definitions suggest that a <u>project is a unique occurrence of a series of tasks (i.e. building a mall, remodeling a house, opening a store site, etc.)</u>.

Advanced Process Improvement methods discussed in this book, such as Lean, Six Sigma and Simple P^2I, view and define the above definition of a project as the definition to a task – a large task, but a task nonetheless.

Let's understand projects and tasks under advanced P^2I:
- What is a project? When is one needed?
  - A project is a vehicle by which to assess current condition(s) of concern and device a plan to improve the outcome.
  - A project is needed when the action(s) to improve the existing outcome is unclear.

- What is a task? When is one needed?
  - A task is a predetermined action, or series of actions.
  - A task is needed when the action(s) to improve the existing outcome is clear.

Example 1:
A Risk Management department processes 1,000 claims a year within a specific period of 3 weeks and a base of 3 employees. One of the claims' representatives leaves the organization and now the department is processing 1,000 claims within a 5 week period but with only 2 employees. The department begins to receive customer complaints regarding the processing time for claims. The director needs to make a decision with respected to the actions to solve/improve the current situation. Is this a project or a task?

Example 2:

A Risk Management department processes 1,000 claims a year within a specification period of 3 weeks and a base of 3 employees. The following year, the processing time increases to 5 weeks. No apparent change known to the department has occurred, but the department cannot seem to reduce processing time back to 3 weeks even with their best efforts. The director needs to make a decision. What to do? Is this a project or a task?

The answers to the above examples at the end of the chapter.

Most necessary changes are a combination of tasks and projects. Each is managed in a different way. But, if the task at hand is large, it needs to be broken-down using work breakdown structures (WBS) – a deliverable based hierarchical method of subdividing tasks/assignments into smaller measurable assignments that need to be finished to successfully complete the master task.

Treating a project, under the revised definition, as a task leads to suboptimal solutions that are not sustainable. Have you ever worked on a project, where no matter what you did, things did not get better? If the answer is yes, chances are you treated a project like a task.

In order to successfully complete a project with sustainable results, the project needs to be:

1. Linked to an organizational **need** (i.e. strategic initiative, operations or compliance).
2. Have a steward that is accountable for the project to oversee the process and support with project needs and/or possible barriers.
3. Led by a project manager that is competent in two critical byproducts: *Problem Solving* and *Critical Thinking*.

    Problem Solving is the science of identifying solutions for that which is not known by using critical thinking skills. *(Critical Thinking is the ability to gather observations, distinguish between fact and opinion in order to arrive at sound logic and evidenced decision making.)*

These skills serve to include breakthrough innovation utilizing benchmarking that propose solutions to known industry advancement; and, build-in (with or without technology) monitoring/tracking tools that sustain improved outcomes while the individual(s) affected by the process adapt to the changes.

** Answers to Examples 1 and 2: Example 1 – task; Example 2 – Project**

Chapter 3:

Six Sigma State of Performance

Six Sigma is a state of performance derived from the normal distribution curve in probability and statistics. In order to understand why, let's review basic statistical concepts.

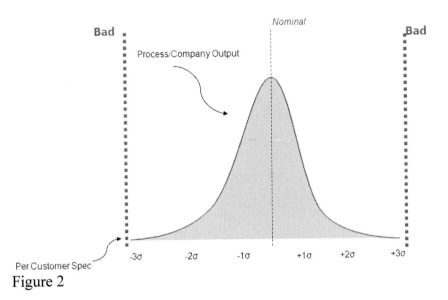

Figure 2

The curve in Figure 2 is a normal distribution curve, or better known as the bell curve. The normal distribution is not the only known distribution in probability and statistics, but it is one of the most commonly used.

The above normal distribution is defined by several characteristics:
- It is a continuous random variable: it takes an infinite number of possible values; usually measurements (i.e. height, weight, time, etc.).
- It is unimodal; increases and decreases by the same magnitude.
- The curve extends indefinitely in both directions, approaching, but never touching, the horizontal axis
- The average (mean) of the distribution resides in the middle of the curve. This is commonly known as the sum of all the numbers divided by the count of the numbers.
- It is symmetrical with respect to the mean. That is, 50% of the area (data) under the curve lies to the left of the mean and 50% of the area (data) under the curve lies to the right

of the mean. If you fold the curve about the average, both sides are exactly the same.

- The area under the curve equal 1. This area is used to calculate the probability of occurrence for an event with a normal distribution.
- The average is important but, alone, does not identify the behavior of data points with respect to its distribution.

> Example1: Data set {1, 9}. The average (mean) = (1+9)/2 = 5.
>
> Example2: Data set {1, 9}. The average (mean) = (5+5)/2 = 5.

Both Examples 1 and 2 have the same average, but the numbers within the respective data sets are drastically different. In Example 1, the average is not representative of the numbers within the data set; but in Example 2, the average is representative of the numbers within the data set.

The difference between the two data points is the degree of disparity between the numbers within the data sets. In Example 1, the numbers are 8 points apart: 9 – 1; where in Example 2, the numbers are 0 points apart: 5-5. This is called the range, and is a measure of variability between the data points in a set of data. This measure of variability is adequate for a data set with a small number of data points, but is insufficient data sets that have large and/or infinite number of data points.

The normal distribution uses a standard deviation as a measure of disparity (variability) from the mean for the data points within the data set. In Greek symbols, this is known as a sigma. The standard deviation calculates the difference between each data point in the data set from the mean, squares each difference to eliminate negative numbers that may cancel each other, sums the squared differences and divides the total by the number of data point. **This calculation is different for estimates of the standard deviation, but is not covered in the scope of this book.**

The distribution ends at third standard deviation, and follows the following:

~ 68% of the area (data) under the curve is within one standard deviation of the mean, to the left or right

~ 95% of the area (data) under the curve is within two standard deviations of the mean, to the left or right

~ 99.7% of the area (data) under the curve is within three standard deviations of the mean, to the left or right

Translating this back into business outcomes/outputs:

If the data in the normal distribution represents the output of a process or company, customer requirements are placed about the curve to determine the difference between the expected (average) behavior of the output and customer requirements. Figure 2, reflects an output distribution where the customer requirements are three standard deviations away from the mean (average). The average is indicated by the dashed line in the middle of the curve titled: *nominal*. The dashed lines at the end of each extreme of the curve titled 'Bad' identify the customer requirements. As you can see, the customer requirements are three standard deviations away from the mean (average).

Using the probability tables for a normal distribution, it is derived that a process with three standard deviations has anomalies (% of data points that fall outside three standard deviations) of 6.68%. That is, 6.68% of the data points fall outside of the third standard deviation. If the customer requirements are at three standard deviations, then you can expect that 6.68% of the outcomes will be deemed unfit for use, or customer dissatisfaction – referred to as **defects** or **defective**. If the product or service is defective then it can be redone to change the outcome to positive; but, the same is not true for a defect. The outcome of a defect cannot be altered.

In business, change is fact of life and is unavoidable. This change is a result of market share changes, economic conditions, etc. It has been quantified as 1.5 standard deviations shift (move) in the mean, and is expected every couple of years.

In the three standard deviation outcome analysis studied above, the change would mean an additional 1.5 standard deviation of products deemed unfit for use, or customer dissatisfaction. See Figure 3.

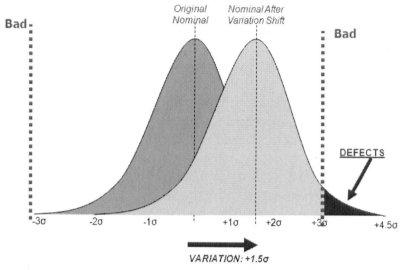

Figure 3

In order to tie the % of defect/defective outcomes to tangible defect/defective outcomes, let's understand the following definitions:

- *Opportunity.* The beginning of every process (macro or micro) is an opportunity to fail or succeed.
- *Defect Rate (DR).* A defect rate is the percentage of 'bad' outcomes/products – outside of customer requirements; thus, unfit for use.
- *Yield.* % of the 'good' products – within customer requirements.
- Yield + DR = 100%

Out of 1 (one) million opportunities, 66,800 are defects (outside customer requirements and unfit for use).

Example, if the opportunities represent dollars then it can be expected that $66,800 out of every $1,000,000 will be lost in a process where the average is three standard deviations (sigma) away from the mean. You can find the process sigma table in Appendix A, using this table, you can determine the process sigma level for a given DR. You simply have to:

- Multiply the DR times 1 Million: DR x 1,000,000 = expected **D**efects **P**er every **M**illion **O**pportunity (DPMO)
- Look up the DPMO value to on the second column within the table and find the value that approximates it
- Look at the correlating process sigma to the left. This process sigma level is how far the average of the observed output fall from the customer requirements

Let's complete the exercise using the 3 sigma analysis we did earlier.

- DR = 6.68% (% expected to fall outside of three standard deviations - sigma)
- Multiply 6.68% x 1,000,000 = 66,800
- Look up 66,800 in the Appendix A table. You can see that the process sigma level associated with the DPMO is 66,800.

AS YOU CAN SEE IN APPENDIX A, A SIX SIGMA PROCESS IS ONE THAT HAS 3.4 DEFECTS FOR EVERY ONE MILLION OPPORTUNITIES.

The Six Sigma methodology studied later in this book aims to reduce the variation in outcome performance such that the average is six standard deviations (sigma) away from customer requirements, and incurs 3.4 defects per every one million opportunities.

Before Variation Reduction

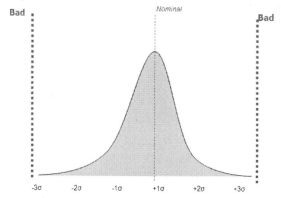

After Variation Reduction

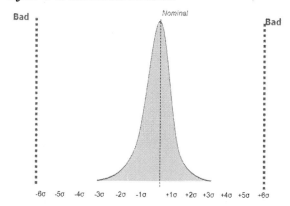

Chapter 4:

Lean Six Sigma Methodology

Chapter 4.1:

Lean Overview

Lean is a set of concepts and tools that exist to identify events/steps within a process that do not add value to the desired outcome for process (waste), but incurs costs and leads to possible defects.

In short, if you can complete a process in three steps, then why do it in ten? As discussed earlier, each step or event in a process is an opportunity to fail or succeed. So, additional steps that are not required increase the likelihood of having a bad outcome while expending additional funds.

LEAN eliminates waste!

Lean does not follow a standard method. Rather, it is a set of tools such as:

- KAIZEN
- Seven forms of Waste
- 5S
- Spaghetti Diagram
- Value Stream Mapping (Value Analysis)
- Takt Time
- Standard Work for Products and Employees
- Kanban
- Mistake-Proofing (Poka-Yoke)
- Push and Pull
- Value added to Non-value added Lead time ratio
- Visual Factory, Management and Metrics

- Workflow Diagram
- Zero Changeover
- Work Balance
- One-Piece-Flow

Some of the concepts and tools listed overlap. But, organizations and/or individuals can use them collectively or independently to drive improvements.

Kaizen is a continuous methodology that involves every level of an organization (from upper management to the front-line workers, inclusive of all levels in between) in order to drive multiple small improvements on a continuous basis that in the end result in innovations that improve:
- Productivity
- Safety
- Effectiveness
- Bottom-line

Kaizen was developed in Japan post World War II. It means Continuous Improvement. Is derived from the Japanese Words Kai and Zen:
- Kai means school.
- Zen means wisdom.

Its purpose is to drive corporate-wide breakthrough thinking as a culture! The events are conducted in a series of work-out sessions with all critical parties (from top management to frontline employees) present. This helps drive improvement QUICKLY!

Kaizen can be used as a method, or the critical tools can be incorporated into the Six Sigma Method to help drive the goals of Lean and Six Sigma jointly: *Reduce Waste and Variation!*

Kaizen is not appropriate in the following circumstances:
- Facility changes and site modifications are required
- Large scale information systems initiatives are needed
- Major Capital Resources are required

- Major investigation is required to identify potential solutions
- Additional focused resources will not accelerate the implementation
- Potential sub-optimization is likely

The following are critical components that must exist for successful integration of Kaizen:
- Leadership – management must lead by example, listen to and implement ideas generated by employees; and, reward positive change behaviors.
- Communication – management must generate transparency throughout the organization. Establish channels of communication that effectively penetrate from management to front-line workforce.
- Teamwork – develop teams that collect and assess ideas and make recommendations for implementation with recognition of idea agents.

Seven forms of wastes
1. *Idle Time* (Waiting) – Time spent waiting, or simply not performing
2. *Unnecessary transport of material* – moving material because of the logistic setup that can be avoided by better organization
3. *Unnecessary Movement (Walking)* – moving non materials resources because of the logistic setup that can be avoided by better organization
4. *Operations/Processing* – Unnecessary steps, or functions, conducted to achieve the same/similar outcome
5. *Inventory* – Products/parts held waiting for use
6. *Overproduction* – Producing more products/parts then are needed
7. *Defects* – Production of bad products/parts that cannot be used, or need rework

5S is a simple tool that helps create and maintain a clean and organized high performance environment that easily distinguishes from common and uncommon conditions in order to reduce defects, costs and maintain a safe work environment.

| Sort | Set in Order | Shine | Standardize | Sustain |

Sort – items should be organized to be easily accessible when needed. Unnecessary items should be **ELIMINATED**. A way to identify if items are properly sorted is to draw a ***Point-to-Point*** (spaghetti) Diagram. A point-to-point diagram is a layout of the workplace/process where the product is tracked for each movement/step conducted. Each of the movements/steps is mapped using arrows. The diagram graphically displays the complexity, or number of steps/moves, needed to complete the process. It also serves as a reference to restructure the pieces/items needed to conduct the process more efficiently. The process in Figure 4, is completed by moving between locations multiple times. There are a total of 35 moves completed to achieve the overall outcome. In a case like this, determine if all the indicated moves are needed, or if they can be reduced/eliminated.

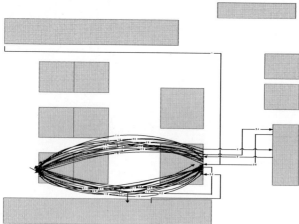

Figure 4

Following are examples of things to sort/eliminate:
outdated, broken, defective, excessive, or simply unneeded items.

Tagging is another known form of sorting. In a tagging exercise, you tag/mark all unneeded or unutilized items. After assessing all items, you place tagged items in a holding area. After a few days (no more than seven), items in holding area are reassessed, and items deemed as unnecessary are thrown away.

"When in doubt, move it out"

Step 1: Tag unneeded items. See Figure 5.

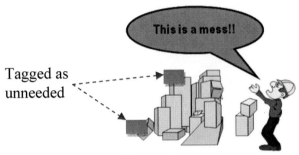

Figure 5

As a rule of thumb: If you have not used it in a year and don't need it for legal reasons, tag it.

Step 2: Separate tagged and untagged items

Step 3: Sort through tagged items – after 5 to 7 days

Step 4: If tagged items are deemed unnecessary, dispose of it.

Step 4: Organize and clean remaining. See Figure 6.

Figure 6

Set in Order (Simplify) – rearrange and properly label the remaining items so that **anyone** can easily find it. When you are setting items in order, design the new layout to minimize walking, bending, zigzagging, or any form of unnecessary movement.

Shine – design a maintenance schedule and structure to ensure safety and cleanliness. This includes maintaining traffic areas clear, machine/equipment maintenance schedule, properly storing hazardous items, devising protocol for spills, trash pick-up or any general messes. In a shine assignment, devise and communicate to employees in order to assign responsibility and accountability as a shared exercise among all employees of the respective areas.

Standardize – devise a plan for maintaining the flow and work environment with the sort, set in order and shine conditions. Be sure to communicate this plan to all employees and set a systematic structure to share the responsibility of maintaining the desired condition(s). This is a plan to make the improved process a *way of life*.

Sustain – establish a vehicle in which to measure that the above conditions or tasks are completed/maintained. Then, stipulate proper action plan in the event protocols are violated. You can do this through schedules and/or scorecards that track the day-to-day outcomes.

Value Stream Mapping (VSM) is a process flow that clearly illustrates the steps with relevant data of the existing value process followed. At the end of a VSM, you should have a single map delineating the critical steps and value process to complete the process at hand; and, identified areas for improvement/opportunity.

VSM has two phases:
- Phase one identifies the existing process with value analysis:
    - Identify the Product
    - Gather Customer Information Demand, Takt Time, Technical Requirements
    - Walk the As-Is Process and Identify Steps and Flow
    - Identify Outputs for each Process Step (Y's)
    - Identify Data Box Categories
    - Cycle Time
    - Throughput Time
    - Yield
    - Number of Shifts
    - Available Time
    - Up Time
    - Populate data boxes based on multiple observations
    - Identify Inventory between steps
    - Identify the number of operators at each step
    - Map the information flow
    - Create timeline
    - Compare value added and non-value added time
    - Identify Improvement Opportunities

Value Analysis is the process of analyzing each process step to determine if it adds value to the process, or if it is a wasteful activity:

Value-Added: VA
Any activity/step that has the ability to change the outcome the customer is expecting (changes form, fit or function. This is what customers are willing to pay for!
Pure Waste: WA

Those activities that are not necessary to deliver customer requirements and do not generate a wow factor.
Required Waste: RW
Those that are not necessary to deliver customer requirements but are either: absolutely necessary to sustain the business or cannot be eliminated due to known constraints (often external). An example is this: billing a customer is not a core need because if they got it for free they would be joyful. But it is a necessity for the business.

- Phase two maps the recommended future state of the process after eliminating waste items to drive improvements:

  o Value-Added Activities: IMPROVE
    Any activity/step that has the ability to change the outcome the customer is expecting (the NEEDs). This is what customers are willing to pay for!

  o Required Value-Added Activities: REDUCE
    Those that are not necessary to deliver customer requirements but are either: absolutely necessary to sustain the business or cannot be eliminated due to known constraints (often external). An example is this: billing a customer is not a core need because if they got it for free they would be joyful. But it is a necessity for the business.

  o Non-Required Non-Value-Added Activities (Pure Waste): ELIMINATE
    Those activities that are not necessary to deliver customer requirements, and do not generate a wow factor.

Example: Your objective is to get to work on time; analyze the following:

1) You wake up
2) You realize you ran out of coffee and really need it because you are going to have a long day and don't even know if you'll have time for lunch
3) You take a quick shower and get dressed in a hurry because you have to rush to get to work
4) You stop for a second and get a cup of coffee at a local coffee shop
5) You get to work, but there is no parking because it is after 8am and every space is taken
6) You drive across the street and park in a meter
7) You grab your bag and rush to your office
8) You sit in your desk open your calendar and realize you are 15 minutes late to a critical meeting
9) You walk into the meeting late and excuse yourself
10) You vouch never to go through this again

Now, complete the process map and assign the respective value to each of the process steps.

See Figure 7. A table has been added to the right hand side of the process map. The table has three columns; each column represents one of the three possible value classifications: Value-Added, Pure Waste and Required Non-Value-Added. An "X" is used to indicate the respective process step classification. An arrow is used to map the process step to the respective assigned "X." The following arrows are used as a visual indication of the value classification for the process steps:

······▶ A black dashed arrow represents a **Required Non-Value-Added** process step.

⟶ A solid arrow with a thin arrow head represents a **Non-Required-Non-Value-Added** process step.

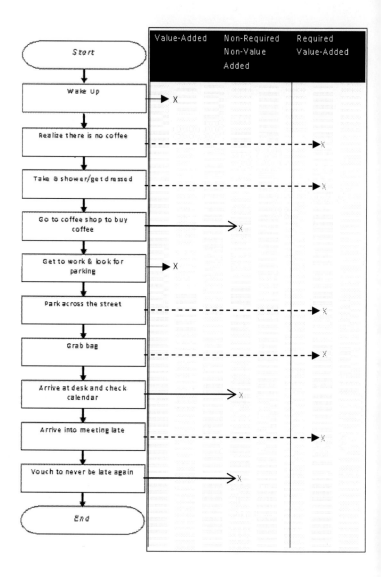

	Value-Added	Non-Required Non-Value Added	Required Value-Added
Start			
Wake Up	X		
Realize there is no coffee			X
Take a shower/get dressed			X
Go to coffee shop to buy coffee		X	
Get to work & look for parking	X		
Park across the street			X
Grab bag			X
Arrive at desk and check calendar		X	
Arrive into meeting late			X
Vouch to never be late again		X	
End			

Figure 7

As you can see from the above example (Figure 7), there are two steps to be improved (Value-Added); three steps that can be eliminated (Pure Waste); and four that can be reduced (Required-Value-Added).

Benefits of Value Analysis through a Detailed Process Map:
- Focuses on the customer.
- Helps you see and understand the flow of material and information in the process.
- Allows for the identification of value-added and non-value-added steps.
- Means working on the big picture, not just individual processes, and improving the whole concept, not just optimizing the parts.
- Provides visibility as well as trains company personnel in seeing the interaction among customer, processes, and suppliers throughout the supply chain.

Takt is the required time to complete the process in order to meet customer specification. *How do you calculate it?*

$$Takt\ Time = Available\ Time \div Average\ Demand$$

The *average demand* is the average number or units to produce, or the number of items to process/service within a set period – customers pre-specify this. *Available time* is the time capacity of the process given the available resources.
As an example, if three hundred clients need visits, and there is one person to make the visits:

σ Available Time = 1 Person x 8 Hours x 60 Minutes = 480 Minutes

σ Average Demand = 300 Visits

Takt Time = 480 Minutes / 300 Visits = 1.6 Minutes/Visit.

This means that a client needs to be visited every 1.6 minutes in order to meet the demand/requirement. Therefore, if the designed process results in client visits every three minutes; then, the process is set up to dissatisfy customers.

Standard Work is the use of a uniform standard through policies and procedures by employees for like procedures.

The analysis for standard work is conducted at the product and employee levels. At the product level, products are manually followed from arrival to departure by one person who is responsible for documenting the start and end times of each activity within the process the product is undergoing. The same product must be followed from beginning to end. The outcome is after a small number of observations (about 10), you can map the variability in steps and handling for like product/service. Thus serves two key purposes:

1. Determine the sublevels that are driving the variability
2. Identify best practices that can be enhanced and implemented as standard procedure using policies and procedures.

See Figure 8.

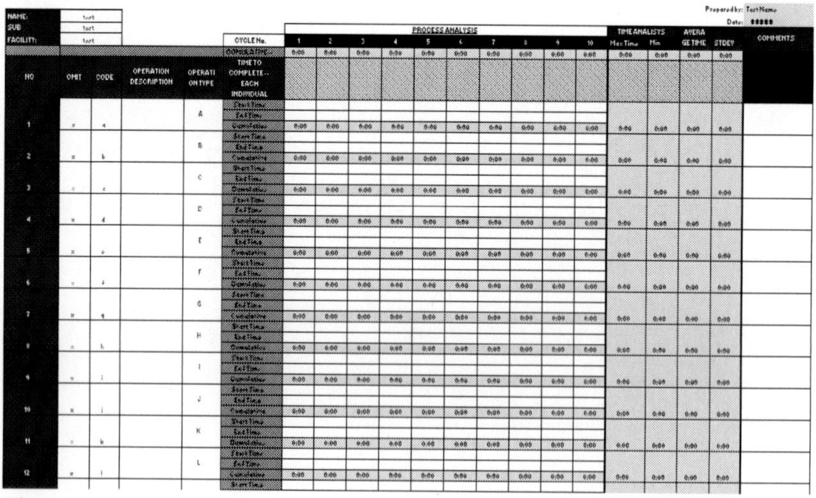

Figure 8

The employee analysis serves to identify process deficiencies and areas of waste for potential improvement by employee in order to drive a standardized process initiative. The best practice can be enhanced and made the standard practice through policies and procedures.

See Figure 9.

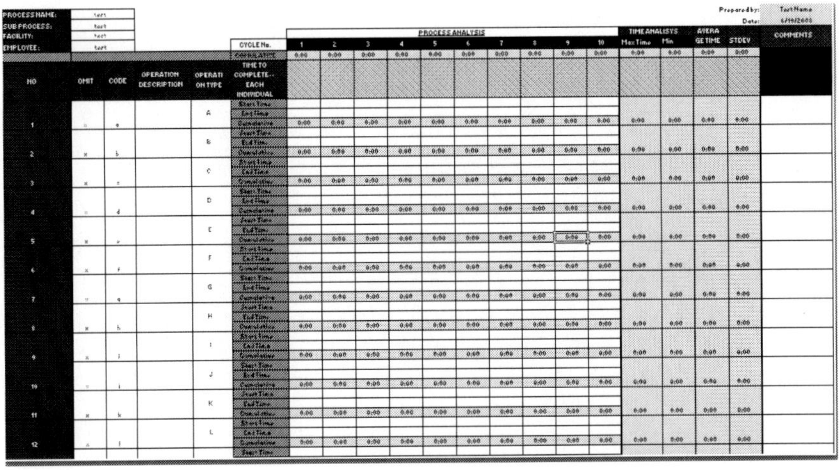

Figure 9

Kanban is a simple parts movement system that depends on cards and boxes/containers to take tangible resources from one work area to another. The essence of the Kanban is that suppliers (warehouse or external) should only deliver components to handle customers or product processing as needed.

Mistake Proofing (Poka-Yoke) is an improvement technology used to prevent defects during customer handling.

Push and Pull
Push is where resource schedules are pushed along based on business growth projections and availability.

Pull is where a system of production and delivery in which nothing is produced by the upstream supplier until the downstream customer signals a need.

Value added to Non-value added Lead time ratio Provides insight on how many value added activities are performed compared to non value added activities, using time as a unit of measure

Work Balance is the concept that activities done in dependency of one another are batch such that the idle time in between waiting for work product is minimized. No one employee should carry the load at any given point in time.

One-piece Flow, or continuous flow, processing is a concept means that items are processed and moved directly from one processing step to the next, one piece at a time. One-piece flow helps to maximum utilization of resources, shorten lead times, identify problems and communication between operations

Chapter 4.2:

Roles and Definitions

they make the project a success. To understand why, it is important to know that there are five levels of people with respect to facing change:

- Those who will make it happen
- Those who will help it happen
- Those who will let it happen
- Those who are slightly against it
- Those who sabotage it

Those who are slightly against or sabotage change are in the minority. Most of them can be convinced to let it happen; and, even help it happen if they understand **why** it is important.

The Six Sigma approach identifies critical people that must be aligned with and support the project in order to minimize the potential for failure due to people related barriers/roadblock – organizational resistance. As, these people have the ability to '*kill*' of '*delay*' a project; six sigma approach refers them as critical stakeholders.

Critical Stakeholders

Champion is the project steward. This person is a Senior Management leader responsible for the success of the project and/or the strategic initiative the project is linked to. This person:

- Approves Projects, Funds Requirements, Allocates Resources, Removes Roadblocks; Makes Final Decisions
- Is not dedicated full time to the project, but is ENTIRELY COMMITTED to the effort, and receives reports. Ideally this is a person *who makes it happen.*

Process Owner(s): one or multiple individuals whom are responsible for the process, in part or whole. Usually know it well with all relevant details and can help with the data gathering and interpretation of data results. The Process owner will be a key help agent throughout the project. These are the more likely to be slightly apposed, or sabotage, change. If the process under review is not owned by one person, but rather a number of people, then all have to be listed as critical stakeholders.

Financial Partner: a person in the finance department, or departmental budget, that is knowledgeable of the global view and can assist in financially quantifying the project(s). This role is important because without a financial partner, the saving cannot be quantified and ROI confirmed.

In developing and deploying a project, a project leader (manager) is similar to an investigator. He/ She are responsible for the investigation's in-depth analytical approach, as well as the involvement of the critical stakeholders and other individuals impacted by the project.

Traditional process improvement conduct what is known as an *inch-deep* and *mile-wide* analysis. This means that a mile-wide range of issues are analyzed for an inch in depth (rigor).

Where, Six Sigma projects are segmented to break-down the focus into smaller, more direct and manageable scope – inch-wide; but, conduct thorough in-depth analysis on the revised scope – mile-deep. Figure 9 shows the analytical difference in approach. Please note that all measurements are shown in inches; and 1 mile = 63,360 inches.

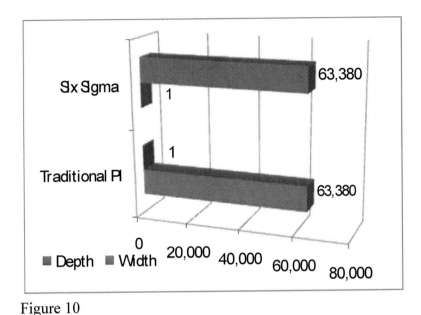

Figure 10

What if the problem is a mile wide? This is a commonly asked question.

In the event that the problem is a mile wide, the Six Sigma approach considers the complexity of the problem and number of possible barriers in order to segment the problem into one advanced project with multiple outcomes or multiple simpler projects with fewer outcomes each. The project lead(s) assignment corresponds to type of project segmentation.

Example:
A retail clothing store has three major lines for sale: Kids, Women and Men. Each of these lines is supported by 5 to 10 different suppliers. Overall, the Vice President of Operations knows based on reports that they have a supplier issue in each of the lines, and has decided to do a major analysis for each of the lines to arrive at solutions because they cannot continue one more year in business with the current problems. This macro scope can be addressed in several ways:

- *Traditional PI*: One large project title 'Supplier Project.' The scope of the projects is to analyze which suppliers for each line are deficient, and begin the process of replacing them.

- Six Sigma Approach: It is unlikely that about 15 to 30 suppliers are deficient. Additionally, it is not known that the issues are exactly the same for each line. In order to identify the issues at hand, a thorough analysis will be conducted for each line. The following projects can be established:
    - One advanced project with three measurable outcomes: % compliance for Kids, % compliance for Women, % compliance for Men; where, each of the outcomes is studied in detail to identify reasons for failure.
    - Three simpler projects are setup each addressing one of the outcomes listed above; where, again, each of the outcomes is studied in detail to identify reasons for failure.

The Six Sigma approach takes the varying levels of complexity and roadblocks into account when assigning project leaders; and, aligns projects to leaders (managers) based on their respective pre-established certified expertise in the six sigma methodology.

Six Sigma **Project Leaders** have the following Criteria:
- Customer Focus
- Interpersonal/Communication Skills
- Technical/Functional Skills
- Leader/Facilitator/Coach
- Boundary-less
- Change Agent/Process Focused
- Confident/Tough/Tenacious
- Project Management Skills
- Has Respect of Associates

The varying levels of Project Leaders are listed below:

Green Belt: leads less political projects with a single outcome or measure to improve, uses simple statistics and does not require the implementation of software or capital investment for gains to be realized.

- REQUIREMENT FOR CERTIFICATION: pass a Green Belt Exam and Complete a Green Belt Project.

Black Belt: leads more political projects with multiple outcomes or measures to simultaneously improve, has higher monetary gain and may require a deeper depth of statistical analysis.

- REQUIREMENT FOR CERTIFICATION: pass a Black Belt Exam, teach 2 Green Belt courses and complete two Black Belt Projects.

Master Black Belt: works with higher profile projects that have a plentitude of complexities; and, is responsible for continuously enhancing the methodology.

- REQUIREMENT FOR CERTIFICATION : Black Belt Certification, Mentor 10+ Black Belts to successful certification and teach 2 Black Belt courses.

There are levels of certification that are not explained within the context of this book because they are transitioning certifications (i.e. yellow belt, brown belt, etc.).

Chapter 4.3:

D-M-A-I-C Overview

There are two forms of Six Sigma methodology:

- *Define-Measure-Analyze-Improve-Control (DMAIC)*: this methodology is the most commonly applied, and is used to improve existing processes in order to achieve a six sigma state of performance

.

- *Define-Measure-Analyze-Design-Validate (DMADV)*: this methodology is often referred to as Design for Six Sigma (DFSS). Companies that are experienced in DMAIC realize that most processes that are designed need to be improved when they get to production/operations. As such, in order to improve the transition, DMADV is implemented to design processes such that they are launched into production/operation with a Six Sigma state of performance.

This book studies the DMAIC methodology in depth.

The DMAIC methodology has a proven data drill-down capability that is based on statistical analysis. This helps achieve the goal within Six Sigma: reduce variation.

What an about Lean Six Sigma?
Lean Six Sigma follows the DMAIC methodology, but embeds lean in order to achieve both waste and variability reduction.

Lean Six Sigma Highlights

Step 1: Define

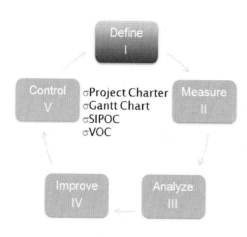

Goal
- Define the project's purpose and scope and get background on the process and customer

Output
- A clear statement of the intended improvement and how it is to be measured
- A high level map of the process
- A list of what is important to the customer

Step 2: Measure

Goal
- Focus the improvement effort by gathering information on the current situation

Output
- Data that pinpoints problem location or occurrence
- Baseline data on current process sigma
- A more focused problem statement

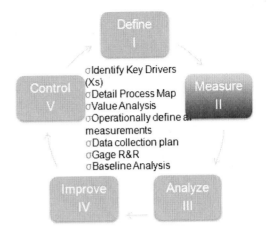

Step 3: Analyze

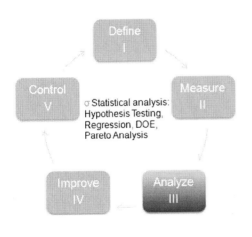

Goal
- Identify deep causes and confirm them with data

Output
- A theory that has been tested and confirmed

Step 4: Improve

Goal
- Develop, try out, and implement solutions that address deep causes

Output
- Planned, tested actions that should eliminate or reduce the impact of the identified root causes

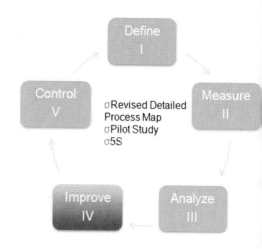

Revised Detailed Process Map
Pilot Study
5S

Step 5: Control

Goal
- Use data to evaluate both the solutions and the plans
- Maintain the gains by standardizing processes
- Anticipate next steps

Output
- Before and After analysis
- Monitoring system
- Completed documentation of results, learnings, and recommendations

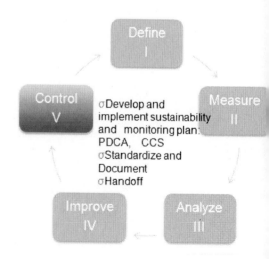

Develop and implement sustainability and monitoring plan: PDCA, CCS
Standardize and Document
Handoff

Chapter 4.4:

Phase 1, Define Phase

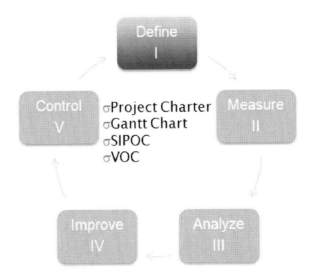

Project Charter

A project charter is a simple living document that identifies who^3 (*who* is the leader, *who* is the champion and *who* are the stakeholders), **what** is/are the target outcomes for improvement, **why** are the outcomes being improved – as linked to the strategy, operations and/or compliance.

A project charter must be approved by the champion and critical stakeholders prior to the project commencing. It is an agreement between management and the expected team that delineates expectations such that there is no misunderstanding.

The project charter is a living document because the information within the document is in constant evolution as the analysis progresses.

Charter				Performance Measures				
Project Name:		Project Type: *(DMAIC, DMADV, SimpleFi, Kaizen)*		Metric	Baseline	Goal	Actual	Goal Met (Y/N)?
Name of Project Leader:	Dashboard Objective:		Reference No.:					
Campus/Location:	Department/Area:	Start Date:	End Date:	Financial Impact				
				Type of Savings	Estimate (initial)		Actual (at Closure)	
Problem Description:				Cost Reduction				
				Cost Avoidance				
				Revenue Enhancement				
				Approval/Result Verification				

Project Scope:		Name & Title	Approval		Result Verification	
The objective of this project is to increase/decrease (type of improvement) ____(process/measure name) from____ (baseline state) to ____ (desired state/goal) by ____ (deadline).			Signature	Date	Signature	Date
		Project Lead Name: Title:				
Team Members:		Sponsor Name: Title:				
Name:	Name:					
Role:	Role:					
Name:	Name:	Mentor (MBB or Name: Title:				
Role:	Role:					
Name:	Name:	Financial Partner Name: Title:				
Role:	Role:					
		Process Owner Name: Title:				

Table 1

Elements of the charter are:

Start and End Dates reflect the dates the charter is signed for approval to begin (Start Date) and the date the charter is signed for approval to close (End Date).

Project Name is the assigned name of the project for which the project charter is being developed.

Project Type examples are: DMAIC, DMADV, LEAN (Kaizen) and Simple P^2I

Project Leader is the person responsible for managing/leading the project to successful completion—this is the Simple PI/Green/Black Belt Leader or Candidate.

Dashboard Objective stated the key initiative within strategy, operations and/or compliance the project supports.

Location/Campus is the exact facility or facilities being covered/affected by the project.

Department/Area are the departments and/or areas of the process for which the project is being conducted.

Problem Description is a detailed delineation of the issues resulting from the underperforming outcome(s). This is not a section to state what is wrong, but, rather, to indicate the impact as a result of that which is not working.

Example: *Wrong statement* - there are not enough employees. *Correct* Statement – the process is incurring large backlog of work and we are no longer within customer compliance; even if this, in perception, is due to lack of enough employees.

Outcome Metrics are the outcomes that must be improved by the end of the project. A baseline (beginning state), and goal (desired end state) and actual (actual end state) must be listed.

Team Members The group of individuals that will support the project lead and stakeholders in successfully completing the project.

Project Scope is one sentence that summaries the entire project. It consists of five key elements:
- Direction (decreased or increased)
- Metric – the name of the metric by which the project's success is measured.
- Baseline – State of the metric at the beginning of the project.
- Goal - Expected state at the end of the project.
- Deadline – Expected completion date for the project.

Example: The objective of this project is to *Increase (Direction) Customer Satisfaction Scores (Metric) from 50% (Baseline) to 90% (Goal) by December 15, 2012 (Deadline).*

Financial Metric lists the financial metrics by which the project's return on investment will be calculated. This should be identifies in the same form as the outcome metrics: current, goal and actual.

Gantt Chart

A **Gantt Chart** graphically displays a clear timeline for completing the phases within the DMAIC methodology in order to complete the project by the deadline indicated in the project scope.

Deadlines for the respective phases

	Define End Date	Measure End date	Analyze End Date	Improve End Date	Control End Date
Define					
Measure			The arrows indicate the date assigned to the respective phase within the methodology (i.e. the complete the Measure Phase by such date as indicated by the second column.		
Analyze					
Improve					
Control					

Table 2   Phases to be completed

As you can see in Table 2, a Gantt Chart is a graphical representation of all the phases to be completed, and the respective deadlines. The first column lists all the phases to be completed. The first row lists all the deadlines that are to be assigned to the respective phases listed in the different rows of the first column.

Then, for each row, use an arrow, as shown in Table 2, to indicate the date by which the specific phase is scheduled to be completed. It is possible to have less date columns than rows. This would be the case if multiple phases have the same deadline. It is common practice to revisit each phase within the methodology, but it is expected that the phases initially be completed by the indicated deadline.

Always remember that a Gantt Chart is necessary because it helps visually track the progress of the project. This same tool can be used outside of the DMAIC methodology by changing the content within the rows to the respective tasks or items that need to be completed.

It is common practice to create additional sub rows to assign deadlines to the tools that are to be completed within each of the phases.

SIPOC Analysis

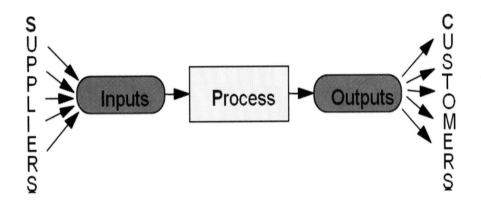

A SIPOC is Supplier-Input-Process-Output-Customer analysis that provides a bird's eye view of the process. It helps place the macro focus of the process into perspective by providing answer to questions like:

- Why does this process exist?
- What is the purpose of this process?
- What is the outcome?

It is a high level process mapped by answering the following questions:

Who are the
Suppliers that provide what
Inputs needed to be *Processed* in order to
generate what *Outputs* to be
received by which *Customer?*

Suppliers can be vendors, departments or specific groups. They are the originating source to the process. Without what the suppliers input, the process is not possible.

Inputs are the parts, documents or simply items provided by the supplier(s) that are needed to complete the process.

Suppliers and Inputs can be identified by asking some or all of the following question:

- Where does the information or material you work on come from? Who are your suppliers?
- What do they supply?
- Where do they affect the process flow?
- What effect do they have on the process and on the outcome?

Process is the high level, "big picture," that provides a global understanding of the overall process and boundaries. It is usually no more than 4 to 7 steps:

- What happens to each input?
- What conversion activities take place?

Outputs are the products or outcomes of the process that are received by the customer of the process:

- What product does this process make?
- What are the outputs of this process?
- At what point does this process end?

Customers are:

- Recipients to the products or outcomes of the process
- Affected parties by the use of the products/services
- Process/Product/Service stakeholders

These definitions are pertinent to the process, and not necessarily the entire organization. As such, it is possible that a middle department finds itself with suppliers and customers consisting of the same personnel.

SIPOC Example

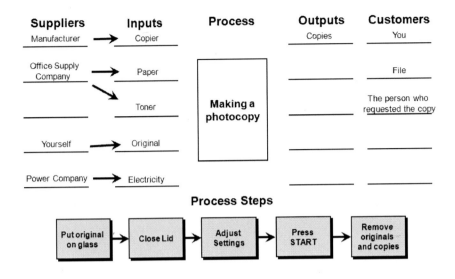

Suppliers	Inputs	Process	Outputs	Customers
Manufacturer →	Copier		Copies	You
Office Supply Company →	Paper			File
	Toner	Making a photocopy		The person who requested the copy
Yourself →	Original			
Power Company →	Electricity			

Process Steps

Put original on glass → Close Lid → Adjust Settings → Press START → Remove originals and copies

Why is it necessary to complete the SIPOC?

The SIPOC is necessary in order to understand the "big picture," boundaries and avoid common project mishaps such as:

σ "Scope Creep," as the boundaries are defined upfront.

What is Scope Creep? Have you ever worked on a project where you had people asking you to please incorporate 'this' or 'that' with respect to their problem? Scope creep is when the project scope grows past its intended objective because 'things' keep coming up. It's addressing world peace in one project.

How do I know if it is scope creep or just addressing customer issues? Simple, you should always inquire and address customer **NEEDS**, as we will discuss later in the Voice of the Customer discussion. You should stay away from gathering and trying to apply suggested solutions. Rather, take the voice of the customer for the respective project boundary and analyze all voice of the customer collectively. This will prevent you from over-reacting to one customer's voice, as the general voice is what will be reflected from the voice of the customer analysis. Using the previously mentioned example, if someone came up to you and asked you to address a communication issue with respect to the department and procurement, you would look at the 'big picture' and realize that the boundary does not deal with that part of the process. Rather, only

the process between procurement and risk management is under the scope of the said project.

σ Isolated areas of improvement, as the high level process are identified.

What is an isolated area of improvement? It is when you improve a process step or a series of process steps instead of the entire process. Using the earlier example, it would be like optimizing the risk management department with respect to the insurance verification without addressing the procurement piece of the process. Isolated areas of improvement generate suboptimal solutions.

σ Customer assumptions, since the SIPOC generates a focus on customer segments that are interviewed through a Voice of the Customer ("VOC") Analysis. (This will be discussed in detail later in the book.)

One of the challenges of the SIPOC is the reality that most people **DO NOT** think in terms of a process; rather, they tend to see things as isolated events. Even once they believe they have learned a better way and are thinking in terms of a process, in reality, they are likely not to be thinking in such terms at all.

Voice of the Customer (VOC) Analysis

The Voice of the Customer VOC analysis is one of Six Sigma's renowned tools. It is critical because it identifies the core **NEEDs** across all customer segments and translates them into technical requirements known as **Critical to Quality ("CTQ")**. The remaining phases are founded on the CTQ. Therefore, without this measure, the project cannot move forward.

Step 1: Identify the customer segment.

The customer segments are the customers identified in the SIPOC analysis under the customer section. It is possible that by conducting the VOC additional customers are identified. If this occurs, the identified customers should be added as a customer to the SIPOC.

Step 2: Determine how many people to interview for each segment.

For each customer group identified in step 1, which should match those in the SIPOC, identify how many **people (n)** you need to interview. This is dependent on the number of people available to be interviewed, confidence level, degree of variability, and precision.

Confidence level is the probability that the accurate response for the entire level will be within your sample/interview. For example: a 95% confidence level indicates that out of 100 interviews, 95 will have the accurate response that would be obtained from interviewing the entire population.

Degree of variability describes the uniqueness in attributes of the population. Large or small values indicate a high level of uniqueness, as the majority of the population does or does not share the attribute. A 50% degree of variability is the largest, as it indicates that 50% of the population does not share the attribute. For example: assume you are performing an interview on a group of physicians in which it is important to capture the opinion of an anesthesiologist. If 50% of the physicians are anesthesiologists, then your degree of variability is 50%.

Precision is a percentage that describes the desired level of accuracy for the respective value within the population. For example: you are performing a survey to determine the percentage of nurses that disagree with a unit policy within a specific hospital and have decided to sample nurses within a specific unit. If the sample has a precision of 5% and the results indicated that 70% of the nurses disagree with the policy, then it can be concluded that if the entire population of nurses had been surveyed, the actual percentage of nurses that disagree with the policy are between 65% and 75%. That is, 70% +/- 5%.

The **standard formula** for a 95% confidence level with a 50% degree of variability, which is standard, is:

$$n = \frac{N}{(1+ (N \times p^2))}.$$

N = Total number of people available to be interviewed

p = Desired precision level
Adopting the nurse example used in the description, if the total number of possible nurses to interview within the unit were 100, then the sample size for a desired precision level of 5% is as follows:

$n = 100 / (1 + (100 \times (5\%^2))) = 80$

Step 3: Determine the type of VOC to be collected for each customer segment.

First, decide which category(ies) of VOC is appropriate for each customer segment. There are two main categories of VOC that can be collected and analyzed:

- Reactive – originates with the customer. These may be seen in the following types:
  - Customer complaints
  - Return information
  - Contested payment
  - Technical support calls
  - Customer service calls

- Proactive – originates with the business and is aimed at gathering proactive information to improve the process outcome. These may be seen in the following types:
  - Interviews
  - Focus groups
  - Surveys
  - Data gathering during visits or calls

Next, identify the specific type of VOC to be collected for each customer segment.

The most effective methods of proactive VOC are: interviews and focus groups

Individual Interviews: One-on-one interviews in person or by phone.

Pros
- Effective in generating new ideas
- Get innuendos
- Read into the interview for further information
- Clear compliance with instructions

Cons
- Time consuming
- Costly
- Difficult to analyze in conjunction with other sources of VOC
- May cause bias

Group Interviews: A group of 7 to 10 people from like segment areas/customers will gather to discuss limited key issues in person.

Pros
- Effective in generating new ideas
- Get innuendos
- Read into the interview for further information
- Clear compliance with instructions

Cons
- Costly
- Difficult to analyze in conjunction with other sources of VOC
- May cause bias

Focus Groups: A group of 7 to 10 people from cross segment areas will gather to discuss limited issues with no more than 3 questions per 2 to 4 hour time segment.

Pros
- Cross reference VOC from market segments
- Reduce gap between company/organization and market segments
- Synergy is able to stimulate positive ideas to create breakthrough thoughts
- Good source for open ended comments

Cons
- Highly emotional environment
- Prior segment knowledge is needed
- Opportunity for open conflict

Step 4: Identify the individuals or groups of people to be interviewed. This only applies to those collecting proactive VOC through interviews, focus groups and/or surveys.

For interview and focus groups, randomly select the actual individuals to be interviewed, by having an external party select the names or write the names of the individuals in slips and place them in a box. Then, draw the number of slips indicated from the sample size calculation.

Create a table with the list of individuals selected and indicate their contact information such as department/area, phone number and email.

For surveys, determine the groups of people that will be reached and the vehicle of communication (i.e. email, live survey, postal service.)

Step 5: Compose the questions that will be asked during the VOC data collection. This only applies to those collecting proactive VOC through interviews, focus groups and/or surveys.

The questions may be tailored specifically to the group being interviewed, but the answers should satisfy the following general questions:

- What is wrong with the process from the individual's perspective?
- What is considered a bad product / service?
- What are critical outcomes to the process? Rank the outcome by order of importance.
- How does that affect the individual's job function?
- If they could have the process as they desire, how would it be?

Step 6: Finalize and conduct VOC.

Prepare a spreadsheet of the VOC plan to enter raw VOC comments. If data collection will be used as the type of VOC, specify the data collection plan and describe the question(s) the data will answer. Also, describe how the data will yield the answers to the desired questions.

Table 3 illustrates a template for a VOC plan.

Customer Segment	No. of People	VOC Type	Raw VOC
Segment 1			
.			
.			
.			
.			
.			
Segment n			

Table 3

Please follow the guidelines below when conducting the VOC:

1. Briefly explain the project.
2. Explain the improvement concept.
3. Establish the groundwork: The purpose is to determine customer needs, not jump to conclusions and commit to solutions.
4. The purpose is to ESTABLISH AND ALIGN CUSTOMER NEEDS.

Step 7: Analyze the VOC.

Once you are ready to analyze the VOC, you may use one of two main analyses:

1. Affinity Diagram
2. Kano Model

An **Affinity Diagram** is used to group large numbers of comments/raw VOC in order to identify the affinity across comments, and arrive at the key recurring needs across customers.

Benefits: Inspires breakthrough thinking, helps identify data patterns, etc.

It is important to use an affinity diagram when the data being collected is qualitative, has complex problems, and if the data needs organization.

Step 1: Place raw comments on note cards or cut them into slips from a simple computer printout.

Step 2: Gather all or some of the team members to analyze the data.

Step 3: Place all data from all customer segments together.

Step 4: Begin placing the comments into "like" groups until the groups can no longer be consolidated.

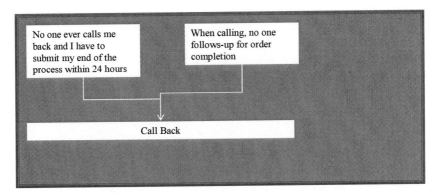

Figure 11

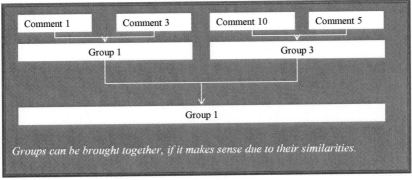

Figure 12

Kano Model is a framework for classifying customer requirements by identifying process characteristics and then prioritizing requirements based on three core classifications:

- **Must Have:** Things expected out of the process or product. Usually people don't even think about this, they simply expect it. These are the core needs customers are willing to pay for.
- **More is Better:** These are things that customers will identify as wanting more of. It is important to address, but not as critical as the "must have."
- **Delighter:** These are the WOW factors. If they are there, the customers are impressed. But in its absence, they won't notice the difference.

In order to conduct the Kano Model follow these steps:

Step 1: Convert all customer comments into requirements.

Comment: "I hate walking into a dark conference room and not being able to turn on the lights."
Requirement: Lights

Step 2: Place into framework.

Category	Must Have	More is Better	Delighter
Lights	Turn on without fail	Brighter	Auto sensor for on and off

Table 4

Step 3: Prioritize requirements based on Kano category. That is, for the list of customer requirements, prioritize the needs giving in the following form:

- Must Have (Highest Priority)
- More is Better (Second Highest Priority)
- Delighter (Third Highest Priority)

In any process, you can expect customers to be satisfied if you cover the customers' core **NEEDS**. Issuing the above prioritization structure increases customer satisfaction because the needs are prioritized and addressed as such.

Step 8: Identify the Critical to Quality(s) (CTQ).

As mentioned earlier, CTQs are core customer requirements. It is, therefore, critical that you can measure the core needs in order to determine if they are being satisfied. But, most CTQs are qualitative measures, and, therefore, not easy to measure for performance. With this said, qualitative needs have to be converted to quantitative needs. That is, un-measurable outcomes have to be converted to measurable outcomes. A **CTQ Tree** can be used to convert qualitative CTQs to quantitative CTQs.

How do I do this?

Step 1: List the qualitative **needs** as identified in the VOC.

Step 2: Identify the drivers of the qualitative CTQ by asking the **'what'** question. For instance, assume a customer identifies that on-time delivery is critical, how do you measure on-time delivery? You have to break it into finer detail. By asking the 'what' question, you would get to the 'on-time delivery of *what* is critical?' Answer: training materials and books have to be delivered on time.

This question leads to identifying the specific products or services for which it is critical to be on time or have on time delivery.

Step 3: Identify the specific requirement(s) for the drivers. Now that you know 'what' is critical, you have to determine **'when'** it is achieved.

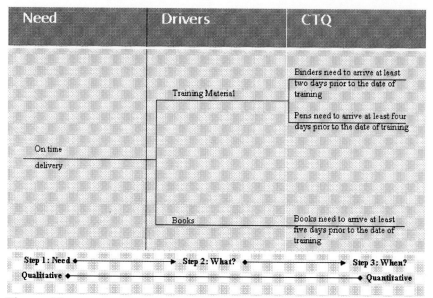

Need	Drivers	CTQ
On time delivery	Training Material	Binders need to arrive at least two days prior to the date of training
		Pens need to arrive at least four days prior to the date of training
	Books	Books need to arrive at least five days prior to the date of training

Step 1: Need ←———————→ Step 2: What? ←———————→ Step 3: When?
Qualitative ←————————————————————————→ Quantitative

Figure 13

Key outcomes of the VOC include:
- Identify changing customer requirements.
- Identify technical specifications for customer requirements.
- Identify customer dissatisfactions such as problems or unfulfilled needs.
- Drive a customer focused process to yield optimal output.

Before collecting the VOC, it is important to develop a plan. Ask yourself the following questions: 1. What type of VOC identifies the critical driving issues? 2. What is the plan and structure for capturing and analyzing the VOC?

VOICE OF THE CUSTOMER (VOC) ANALYSIS SUMMARY

Step 1: Identify the customer segment.

Step 2: Determine how many people to interview for each segment.

Step 3: Determine the type of VOC to be collected for each customer segment.

Step 4: Identify the individuals or groups of people to be interviewed. This only applies to those collecting proactive VOC through interviews, focus groups and/or surveys.

Step 5: Compose the questions that will be asked during the VOC data collection. This only applies to those collecting proactive VOC through interviews, focus groups and/or surveys.

Step 6: Finalize and conduct VOC.

Step 7: Analyze the VOC.

Step 8: Identify the Critical to Quality(s) (CTQ).

A template for this tool is available within the CD enclosed in this book.

By the end of Define Phase, you should be able to describe:

- Why is this project important?
- What business goals must the project achieve to be considered successful?
- Who are the players on the project (sponsors, advisors, team leader, team members)?
- What limitations (budget, time, resources) have been placed on this project?
- What key process is involved (including its Suppliers, Input, Outputs, and Customers)?
- Who are the stakeholders, and how you will communicate with them?
- ***What are the customer requirements or specifications - CTQ?***

Chapter 4.5:

Phase 2, Measure Phase

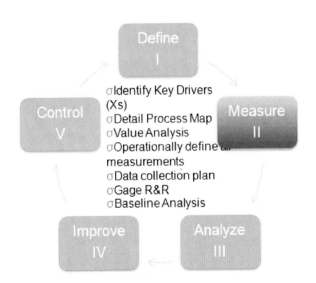

The advantage Lean Six Sigma has over traditional process improvement is the constant drill-down capability.

By the end of the define phase, the project leader has a preliminary business case supporting the project. Next, the business case must be finalized by identifying the possible core drivers that impact the CTQ, and collecting supporting data on the state of all relevant metrics (i.e. Core Drivers and CTQ).

Identify Core Drivers

What are drivers?

A driver is a form of a leading indicator. It reflects a signal to come. As an example, losing your job is an indication that you may not be able to pay your bills in the future.

The CTQ identified in the Define phase is a lagging indicator that follows, or is impacted by, the performance of the core drivers; where, the core drivers are an indication of the outcome of the CTQ.

The following questions can help identify drivers....
1. What is it that makes or breaks the CTQs?
2. What can be changed or improved to get the CTQs to the desired condition?

CTQ and the drivers can be expressed in a simple math formula:

$$Y = X_1 + X_2 + X_3$$

The value of the "Y" depends on the value of the "Xs." "Y" is known as a dependent variable because its value is dependent of the value of the Xs.

Example, if X1 = 1, X2=0 and X3 = 10 then Y = 11.

In this example, "Y" represents the CTQ; and, the "Xs" symbolize the drivers. This book will use the term "Y" interchangeably with "CTQ;" and "X" with drivers.

One or multiple of the following tools can be used to identify core drivers:
- Voice of the Customer (as we saw in Chapter 4.4)
- Cause and Effect Diagram
- Detailed Process Map
    - Process Flow Chart
    - Cross Functional Map
    - Value Stream Map – See Chapter 4.1
- Process Flow Analysis – See Chapter 4.1
- Gage R&R
- Employee Process Flow – See Chapter 4.1
- Failure Mode Effect Analysis (FMEA)

Voice of the Customer often identifies, or signals, possible drivers disguised as something that's needed or wanted.

Cause and Effect Diagram is also known as a "Fishbone" or "Ishikawa" Diagram. The purpose of this diagram is to graphically illustrate the potential causes for a given effect.

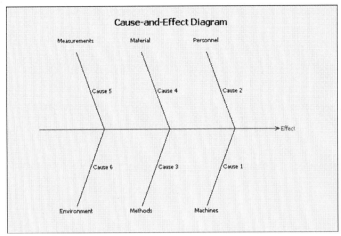

Figure 14

The center line is the effect (outcome) whose state is the result of the causes indicated in the branches. In the scope of DMAIC, the centerline is the CTQ and the causes identified within the branches are potential drivers.

The branches represent standard areas that help brainstorm for possible drivers that may otherwise be overseen. There are two standard types of labels for the branches:
1. *6M:* Manpower (Personnel), Machines (equipment/systems), Methods (procedure), Material (Resources), Measurement, and Mother Nature (Environment).

2. *4Ps:* Policy, Procedures, Plant and People.

This exercise is used exclusively to identify <u>failures</u>, NOT solutions. Solutions will be identified in the Improve Phase. See the following example in order to recognize an **incorrect** Cause-and-Effect diagram.

Incorrect Cause-and-effect Example

Hypothetical Hospital of the Americas has been experiencing a high denial rate for their expected reimbursements. This has lead to a sharp decline in cash flow. The hospital has decided to undergo a Six Sigma Project to decrease denials for their main admitting point. The effect identified is **Denials**, <u>which is the CTQ</u> and now the potential Xs that drive the CTQ need to be identified. Using the 6M methodology (sticking to **M**achine, **M**anpower, **M**easurement, **M**ethod, **M**aterial, and **M**other Nature, from our original Cause-and-Effect Diagram), the figure 14 was generated.

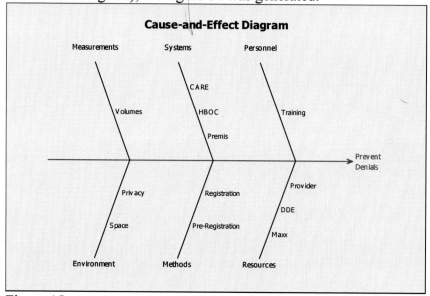

Figure 15

As shown, some potential causes for failure are registration, training, care and space. Notice how all items listed are points where the process can fail and lead to a denial. **No solutions are offered**. Now see at Figure 15.

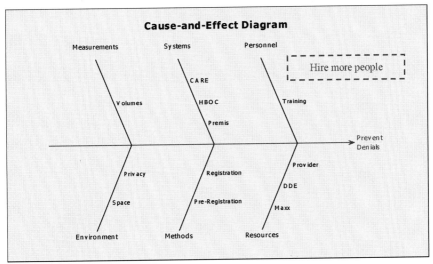

Figure 16

Under personnel, the dashed box identifies a misfit cause. That is, "hire more people" is not a potential failure point; rather, it is an offered solution. Stay away from these types of mistakes. Again, the Cause-and-Effect diagram is used to graphically identify potential failure points in the process, not to list solutions.

Detailed Process Maps are valuable tools in understanding the current process and/or problem condition(s). It is a graphical representation of the process flow that indicates the inputs to each major process step (as identified in the SIPOC).

The basic shapes used to map a process flow are shown in Figure 17.

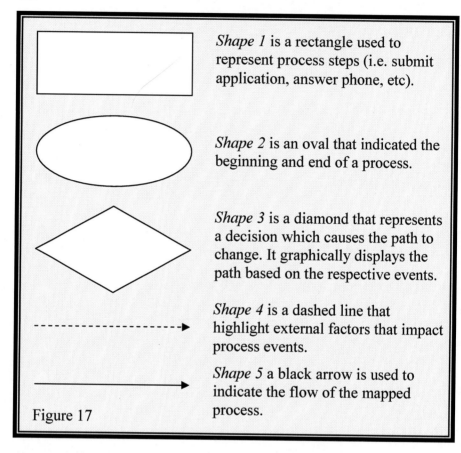

Shape 1 is a rectangle used to represent process steps (i.e. submit application, answer phone, etc).

Shape 2 is an oval that indicated the beginning and end of a process.

Shape 3 is a diamond that represents a decision which causes the path to change. It graphically displays the path based on the respective events.

Shape 4 is a dashed line that highlight external factors that impact process events.

Shape 5 a black arrow is used to indicate the flow of the mapped process.

Figure 17

There are numerous types of process maps, but this book will identify three commonly used in Lean Six Sigma:
1. Process Flow Chart
2. Cross Functional Map
3. Value Stream Map

A *Process Flow Chart* is a visual representation of the steps/events carryout in order to achieve an outcome. This form of mapping is usually limited to the basic shapes identified in Figure 16. This type of mapping is good for highlevel displays of a process such as the SIPOC, and/or processes within a single unit or functional area. Cross functional interaction is displayed as a rectangular box stating "submit to department X" and another stating "give backto department Y."

In the even that a process stems across and impacts numerous department, it is valuable to visually indicate the department within which each process step falls. This helps visually identidy the critical departments to the process as well as the spectrum of invlovement across all departments; among other thing. This form of maping is called **Cross Functional Mapping**.

As you can see in Figures 18 and 19, the functional areas within which the process spreads are listed as columns or rows. Then each of the process steps are mapped within the respective functional area they occur.

Example: The decision point in the cross functional map in Figure 17occurs within department area 5.

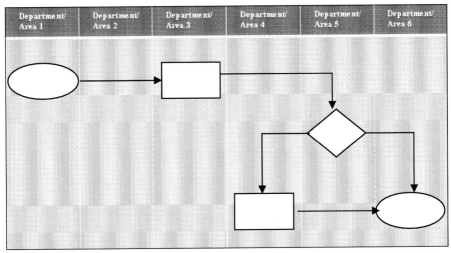

Department/ Area 1	Department/ Area 2	Department/ Area 3	Department/ Area 4	Department/ Area 5	Department/ Area 6

Figure 18

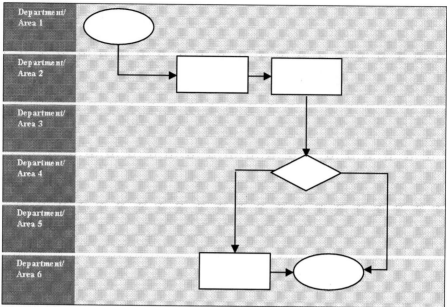

Department/ Area 1	
Department/ Area 2	
Department/ Area 3	
Department/ Area 4	
Department/ Area 5	
Department/ Area 6	

Figure 19

Value Stream Map is explained within the Lean Chapter 4.1. It is important to note, though, that this tool can be interchangeably used with the Process Flow Analysis explained in the Lean Chapter.

A **Gage R & R** is a <u>repeatability and reproducibility</u> **study that** "gages," the consistency within and across output sources.

"If you cannot measure, you cannot improve." – Taguchi

Six Sigma's proven success is in large due to its substantiated results. It is not a subjective format for random ideas. Rather, it is a **structured data driven methodology**. As such, one of the primary focuses is the <u>quality of data</u> collected.

Simple! *Garbage In = Garbage Out!*

Often, management decisions are made on data streams for which the data source has never been tested for reliability. If the data going into a report is inaccurate, all the information derived from that raw data is, by default, erroneous and misleading. If decisions are made on poorly founded data, these decisions are likely to be inadequate, or simply incorrect.

For this reason, a Gage R & R is critical!

What is repeatability?

Repeatability is <u>consistency within individuals</u> or machines to generate the same data time after time. As an example, if Mary calculates OR starting time, and out of ten times she generates the same answer, then she is repeatable.

Repeatability simply means the ability to consistently produce the same type of predictable results. However, this <u>does not</u> mean the results are correct. You can incorrectly measure the same item 100 times. But even if you are consistently wrong, your results are still repeatable. It's the fact that you're getting the same results that repeatability focuses on, not the actual results.

What is reproducibility?

Reproducibility is consistency <u>across</u> individuals or machines to generate the same data time after time. It differs from repeatability like this: in the previous example we were only dealing with Mary. But now, if <u>Mary and Joe</u> (two people) calculate OR starting time, and out of ten times, they both generate the same answer, then they have reproducibility.

Reproducibility simply means the ability to consistently reproduce the same type of predictable results <u>across multiple measurement sources</u> (people or machines). This, again, does not refer to the accuracy of the result. Two, Three, or more people can incorrectly measure the same item 100 times. But even if they are all consistently wrong, the results are still reproducible because they're the same.

Simple note:

Repeatability – consistency in results for <u>a single</u> measuring source
Reproducibility – consistency in results across <u>multiple</u> measuring sources

<u>Gage R & R Example</u>

| Billing Clerk 1 | Billing Clerk 2 | Billing Clerk 3 |

Figure 20

Each Billing Clerk in Figure 20 is responsible for billing corporations for days of service. If every time Billing Clerk 1 bills a corporation, the bill generated reflects a charge of $100 per day of service then clerk one is repeatable. And if every time clerk 1, 2 and 3 send a bill to a corporation, the bill is for $100 per day of service, then all 3 Billing Clerks are reproducible, since they're all getting the same results.

How do I conduct a Gage R & R?

First, let's identify the <u>type of Gage R&R</u> to be conducted.

*Is the data for which the study is being conducted **Attribute** or **Measurement/Continuous**?*

Attribute: Categorical data such as go/no-go, yes/no, white/back.

Measurement/Continuous data is infinite data that can be subdivided into infinitely smaller increments. Some forms of continuous data:

- σ Length
- σ Width
- σ Size
- σ Temperature
- σ Currency
- σ Time

If the data is attribute, then conduct an attribute Gage R & R. Otherwise, conduct a measurement Gage R & R.

Attribute Gage R & R

An attribute Gage R & R is conducted to assess consistency between individuals or machines generating binary data (yes or no, good or bad, correct or incorrect, defect, no defect) that is to be measured to a standard.

Three components are analyzed at this point:

1. Variation within appraiser (the measuring person or machine)
2. Variation between appraiser and standard
3. Variation between appraisers

Now, in order to conduct the Gage R & R, a data collection plan that gathers the data in the format necessary to complete the study and analysis, must be done.

Step 1: Determine how many appraisers conduct the process step that yields the outcome under analysis

Step 2: Determine the product type or scenarios for the units, products, or outcomes under analysis

Step 3: Determine the sample size or number of samples to be collected. The data must be balanced in order to conduct the analysis in Minitab. In other words, each appraiser must have the same sample size for each product type or scenario.

Referring back to the Gage R & R example, there is a total of three appraisers: Clerk 1, 2 and 3. Let us say there are also three account types: Small corporation, large corporation, and independent.

Assuming the clerks process the following number of clients/accounts:

Clerk 1

- Small Corporation: 1,000
- Large Corporation: 500
- Independent: 200

Clerk 2

- Small Corporation: 5,000
- Large Corporation: 300
- Independent: 100

Clerk 3

- Small Corporation: 1,500
- Large Corporation: 500
- Independent: 200

Let's balance the data. Pick the <u>smallest volume of all accounts</u> and clerks and use that volume to determine the sample size to be collected for all accounts per clerk (reason for this is that if you choose a larger volume, that sample size may exceed the total population or volume for the smaller volumes; then it would be impossible to collect the data).

Using the formula from the Voice of the Customer sample size determination:

$$n = \underline{\quad N \quad} / (1 + (N \times p^2))$$

Where N = the population total, or size and p = the desired precision.

(Simple Note: "population" in the field of data has nothing to do with how many people in a city, as we all know; it simply means "data points" in a specific category. So don't think we're trying to stick people in a computer!)

Assuming a 3% precision, the sample size to be collected for small corporation clerk 2 is:

$n =$ ___5,000___ $/ (1+ (5,000 \times (3\%)^2) = roughly\ 909$
(this exceeds the population size of clerk 1, 2 and 3 large corporation and independent)

If the smaller population is chosen (100), then the sample size is:

$n =$ ___100___ $/ (1+ (100 \times (3\%)^2) = roughly\ 52$

This means that 52 samples need to be collected for small corporations, 52 for large corporations, and 52 for individuals from each of the three clerks, leaving us with a total of 156 data points (52 data points multiplied by 3 categories; $52 \times 3 = 156$). We now multiply 156 by the number of clerks (which coincidentally happens to be 3 as well), and we have $156 \times 3 = 468$ samples.

Precision may be adjusted if the sample size is too large. It is <u>not</u> recommended, however, that a sample size per any given scenario per appraiser be less than 20.

Ok, now what do we do with our 468 samples?

Step 4: Meet with the appraisers and review the operational definition for the measurement of study as well as purpose of the project. Once the appraisers understand the purpose of the study and are educated on the data collection mechanism, collect the sample size we determined for each of the appraisers (156 data points) and accounts within the appraisers (52 data points).

Now, for the Gage R & R example, operationally define the account outcome as follows:

Agreed Standard = the accounts must be charged $100 per day of service for small corporations, $1,000 per day of service for large corporations and $50 per day of service for individuals.

Calculation/Formula = Actual amount charged minus expected charge per standard (the previous definition). If this variance (difference) is not equal to zero, then it is not in compliance. The spreadsheet should look as follows assuming a sample size of 5 per appraiser per account: (we'll use a sample size of 5 for simplicity, remember, no less than 20 is recommended)

Sample No.	Appraiser	Account Type	Measurement (Compliance or Noncompliance)	Standard
1	Mary	Small		
2	Mary	Small		
3	Mary	Small		
4	Mary	Small		
5	Mary	Small		
6	Mary	Large		
7	Mary	Large		

Sample No.	Appraiser	Account Type	Measurement (Compliance or Noncompliance)	Standard
8	Mary	Large		
9	Mary	Large		
10	Mary	Large		
11	Mary	Individual		
12	Mary	Individual		
13	Mary	Individual		
14	Mary	Individual		
15	Mary	Individual		
16	Joe	Small		
17	Joe	Small		
18	Joe	Small		
19	Joe	Small		
20	Joe	Small		
21	Joe	Large		
22	Joe	Large		
23	Joe	Large		
24	Joe	Large		
25	Joe	Large		

Sample No.	Appraiser	Account Type	Measurement (Compliance or Noncompliance)	Standard
26	Joe	Individual		
27	Joe	Individual		
28	Joe	Individual		
29	Joe	Individual		
30	Joe	Individual		
31	Peter	Small		
32	Peter	Small		
33	Peter	Small		
34	Peter	Small		
35	Peter	Small		
36	Peter	Large		
37	Peter	Large		
38	Peter	Large		
39	Peter	Large		
40	Peter	Large		
41	Peter	Individual		
42	Peter	Individual		
43	Peter	Individual		
44	Peter	Individual		
45	Peter	Individual		

Table 11

Step 5: Place the completed data in Minitab.

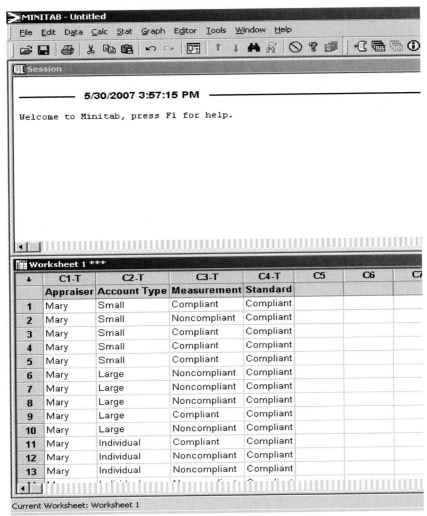

Figure 21

Step 6: Click on Stat (not "Start") > Quality Tools > Attribute Agreement Analysis.

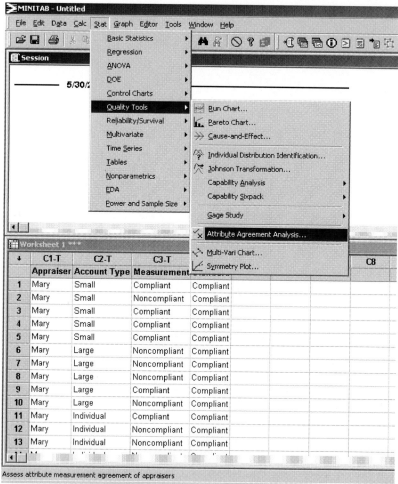

Figure 22

Step 7: Complete the analysis form. Enter the measurement column where the output result is in the **Attribute** field, enter the account type or part numbers in the **Samples** field, enter the clerks or operators in the **Appraiser** field and enter the benchmark or standard in the **Known standard/attribute** field at the bottom of the form. Click 'Enter.'

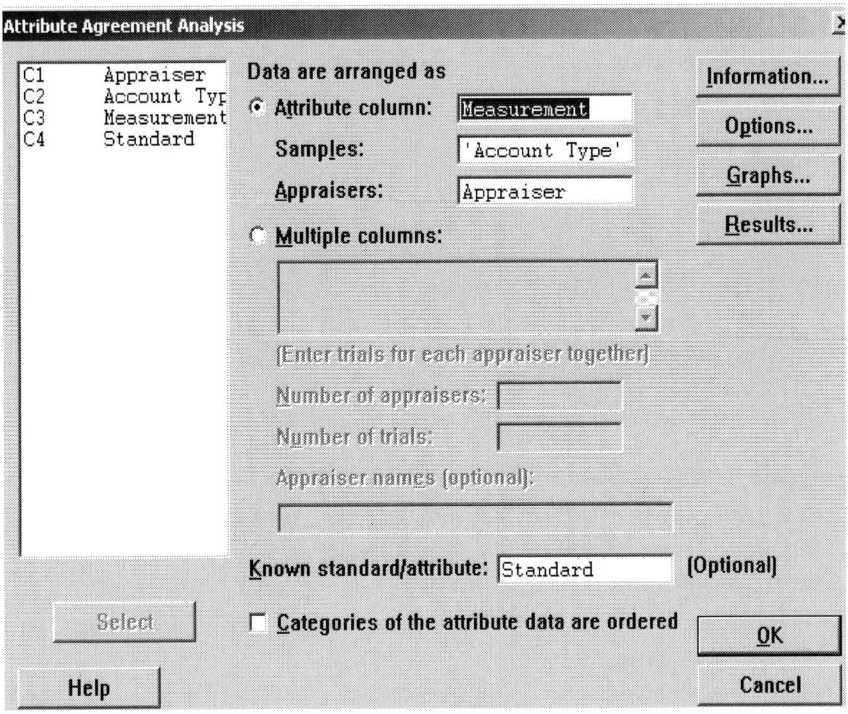

Figure 23

Step 8: Let's interpret the following analysis.

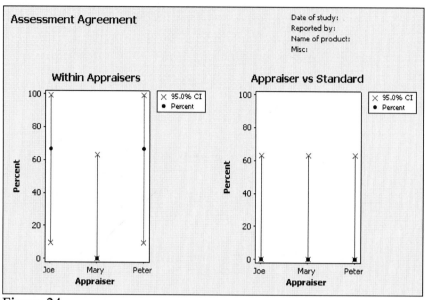

Figure 24

Joe and Peter are about 60% repeatable within them selves and match each other. Mary is not repeatable and does not match Joe or Peter. As per the appraiser vs. standard, as you can see, they are all 0% compliant with the standard. The above represents a measurement problem. All clerks need training on processing accounts to compliance.

Measurement Gage R & R

Steps 1 through 5 from the Attribute Gage R & R we just looked at, apply. The only difference is that instead of capturing that data from the clerks as compliant vs. non-compliant, the actual variance is captured in the measurement column.

Let us revisit the calculation portion of the operational definition offered to the clerks:

Calculation/Formula = actual amount charged minus expected charge per standard. If this variance (difference) is not equal to zero, then it is not in compliance.

This is revised to:

Calculation/Formula = actual amount charged minus expected charge per standard. The difference is documented; not just the "yes" or "no" answer to the question "was it compliant?"

The new data set would look as follows:

Place the completed data in Minitab

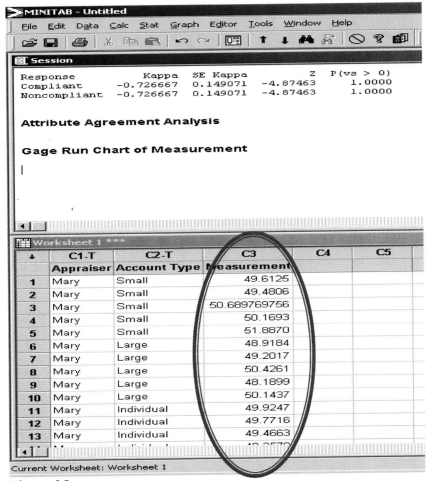

Figure 25

Notice that the data no longer reflects only 'compliant' or 'noncompliant,' rather, actual numbers are indicated.

Now let's click on Stat > Quality Tools > Gage Study > Gage R & R Study (Crossed)

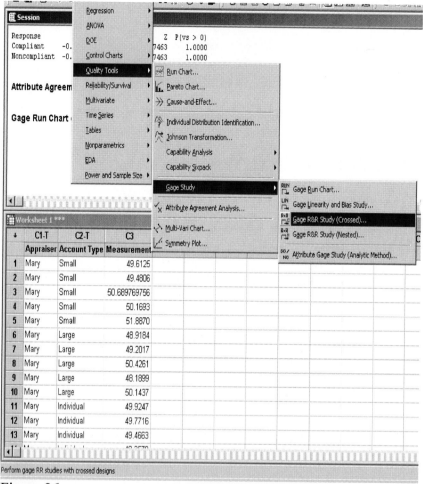

Figure 26

Again, notice that the actual results are indicated.

Next step is to complete the analysis form. Enter the measurement column where the output result is in the **Measurement data** field. Then enter the account type or part numbers in the **Part numbers** field and enter the clerks or operators in the **Operators** field. Select the ANOVA option at the bottom of the form and click "Enter".

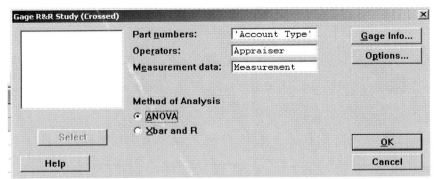

Figure 26

Let's interpret the following analysis:

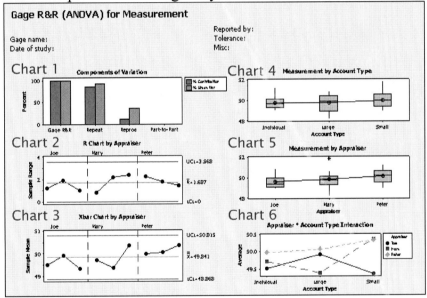

Figure 27

The following outcomes indicate a good Gage R & R:

Chart 1 should be low for the first three bars, but high for part to part. This would indicate that the only variation is from part to part, not in the measurement system. The **chart in Figure 27** indicates that the variation is due to a lack of repeatability and reproducibility; which means the measurement system needs to be standardized for improvement and consistency.

Chart 2 should be within control—all points should be within the control limits. If a point falls outside the control limits, it is said to have special cause of variation.

Common cause of variation is regular, day-to-day variation due to the system and **Special cause of variation** is variation due to something outside the system, a "special" non-common occurrence, which causes a "spike" in the charts.

If chart 2 is within the control limits then the operators are consistent within their measurements and have repeatability. In the above example, the operators have repeatability, as the points are within the control limits.

Chart 3 points should be out of the control limits. This indicates that the part-to-part variation is the main source of variation.

In the above example, the points for Chart 3 are within the control limits. This is an indication that the main source of variation comes from the system, not the part-to-part variation.

Chart 4 indicates the variation from part to part. As you can see from the above example, the output is consistent across parts.

Chart 5 indicated the variation from appraiser to appraiser. As you can see from the above example, there is great variation across appraisers.

Chart 6 should show parallel lines, which would indicate lack of interaction by appraiser. In the above example, these lines are not parallel. This indicates a variation <u>and</u> interaction by appraiser.

In conclusion, the data analyzed has a reproducibility and accuracy problem. Prior to continuing to the remainder of the problem, the Gage R&R should be addressed by improving the measurement system used by the Billing Clerks.

Note: this study is interchangeable with the Employee Flow Analysis within the Lean Chapter 4.1

Failure Mode Effect Analysis (FMEA)

Now that <u>potential</u> drivers have been identified, you need to prioritize. If you have more than three to five drivers, you can use an FMEA to prioritize and identify the critical few that have the greatest impact on the CTQ.

A Failure Modes Effect Analysis (FMEA) is used to identify those elusive, critical few Xs, or driving issues. FMEA is a structured analysis that highlights the potential failure modes for each of the "Xs" (causes), the severity of the failure, and measures how often the failure is likely to occur. Intuitively, a high-risk "X" (a high-risk cause) is one that has a **sever** effect from failure, occurs often and is not readily detected and addressed.

How is an FMEA constructed?

Step 1: (See Table 6 below.)

Critical Parameter	Potential Failure Mode	Potential Effect(s) Failure(s)	S e v	Cause(s)	O C U R	Current Process Controls	D E T	R. P. N.	Recommended Actions	Responsibility & Target Date	Action Results Actions Taken	S e v	O c c u	D e t	R. P. N.
X_1 (Cause 1)															
X_2 (Cause 2)															

Table 6

List all possible causes on the left hand side of the table under critical parameters.

Step 2: For each X (cause), identify all possible failure modes. How can the process step/cause fail to perform? Complete this step in column 2 of Table 6; under "Potential Failure Mode."

Step 3: For each failure mode, identify the effect of the failure. What happens if the failure mode takes place? Complete in column 3 of Table 6. ("Potential Effects Failure")

Step 4: Rate the severity of the failure mode effect identified in column 3. See Table 7 for the severity ratings. Enter the severity rating in column 4. ("SEV")

Severity Ratings

Rating	Criteria: Effect causes/results in _____. [complete the statement from the list below, and assign the appropriate rating to the FMEA table]	
		Bad
10	Physical or emotional injury to a customer or employee	
9	Illegal process step	
8	Product/service unfit for use	
7	Extreme customer dissatisfaction	
6	Partial malfunction	
5	Loss of performance leading to a complaint	
4	Minor performance loss	
3	Minor issues to be fixed with minimal or zero loss	
2	Unnoticeable with minor performance effect	Good
1	Unnoticeable with no effect on performance	

Table 7

Step 5: For each failure mode, identify the possible cause for the failure. What led it to fail? How did the system fail? Complete this in column 7: "Cause(s)"

Step 6: For each failure mode, identify how often this failure occurs. Use Table 8 to rate the occurrence, and enter the occurrence rating in column 8: "OCUR"

Rating	Criteria: This failure occurs _____. [complete the statement from the list below, and assign the appropriate rating to the FMEA table]	
		Bad
10	Daily	
9	Several times a week	
8	Once a week	
7	Once a month	
6	Once a quarter	
5	Once every six months	
4	Once a year	
3	Once every couple of years	
2	Once every few years	
		Good
1	In excess of 5 years	

Table 8

Step 7: For each failure mode, identify the process controls currently in place. Complete this in column 7 of Table 6: "Current Process Controls"

Step 8: For each failure mode, rate the detection possibility. Use Table 9 to rate the detection. Enter the detection rate in column 8 of Table 6: "DET"

Detection Ratings		
Rating	Criteria: This failure is detected as follows: _____. [complete the statement from the list below, and assign the appropriate rating to the FMEA table]	Bad
10	Not detectable	
9	Occasional defect checks are run	
8	Systematic samples and inspections	
7	Census manual inspection that may lead to human error not known	
6	Manual inspection with rework process built in	
5	Monitored with SPC, but manually inspected	
4	SPC with immediate response to out of control points	
3	SCP with 100% response to out of control conditions	
2	Automatic inspections	
1	Defect is obvious and is fixed without affecting the customer	Good

Table 9

Step 9: Calculate the Risk Priority Number and enter it into column 9 of Table 6: "RPN"

The Risk Priority Number (RPN) is the number used to prioritize the Xs/causes of the process.

RPN = Severity Rating x Occurrence Rating x Detection Rating

The highest possible rating is 1,000. This occurs when all ratings are 10s, and would mean that the process has failure modes that can cause physical or emotional damage to a customer or employee, occurs daily, and is not detectable. This number indicates that the Xs with these conditions need to be addressed with the highest priority, as they are a critical driving force (take us to a certain condition) for the process; and thus, they become the focus of the project.

Operational Definition

Once the Core Drivers/Xs have been identified, they need to be operationally defined along with the CTQ.

What is an Operational Definition?

An Operational Definition is a <u>detailed explanation</u> of the standard for a measure and the <u>exact calculation</u> of how to measure the actual performance. It does not leave room for questions or misunderstandings.

The two main components of an operational definition are:

1. <u>Standard</u> – the standard is the stakeholder/customer technical requirement of the performance expectation.
2. <u>Calculation/Formula</u> – the calculation is the exact formula or detailed specification in order to be in compliance with the standard (component #1).

Operational Definition Example

Hypothetical Hospital of the Americas requires all surgeries to begin by 8am but is finding non-compliance with a number of their doctors; they're not meeting this requirement. An operational definition of on-time surgery start needs to be established and all doctors trained such that all involved parties are aware of the standard and measure compliance in the same form.

Standard: All surgeries must start by 8am (But does this mean "patient in room" by 8 am or "incision takes place" by 8 am?)

Standardized (agreed upon) Operational Definition:

Start time = when the patient finally arrives at this assigned room for surgery

Calculation/Formula: Actual "patient in room" time per OR clock
– 8am

The above operational definition makes it clear to all parties that surgeries are to begin by 8am and its on-time compliance will be set by the actual "patient in room" time, <u>as per the OR clocks</u>. Now, misunderstandings as to how, where or when, or by which clock start time is measured on, will not be a source of variation.

Baseline Analysis

Now that the drivers have been confirmed and the measurement system validated, we're ready to collect data in order to understand the base condition of the current measurements (CTQ and Drivers).

Step 1: Determine the sample size for the CTQ based on the population size (Remember, population does not refer to world population. It refers to data amount). The sample size will be the same across all measurements.

Step 2: Determine the data type for each of the Xs and the Y (CTQ).

Step 3: Prepare the data collection sheet. Note that the same rules used for collecting data for Gage R & R apply. For example, if there are 3 shifts or areas, the data to be sampled should be done across all shifts.

Data Collection Example

Department A has 3 **shifts**, 1 CTQ and 4 Xs. The established sample size is 15 (meaning 15 samples need to be collected for each shift). The condition and data value for each of the 4 Xs should be noted. A total of 45 samples would be collected for the CTQ and the setting for each of the Xs noted.

(Simple Note: Try to stay away from interpreting every bit of data to its fullest extent for now. Simply, see how it's being used to operate the charts and move on.)

Step 4: Collect the data.

Step 5: Analyze the data using one or multiple of the following tools:

Pareto Chart is a type of bar chart that aligns categorical data by % impact on the whole. As an example, if you have a medical center that is trying to understand the breakdown of total defects that occur in collection of funds, you can use a Pareto Chart to illustrate the breakdown of the overall defects by category. See Figure 28. Each of the bars represents one of the categories of defects in collections. The first row under the chart indicates the total count per bar/category. The second row indicates the category's respective % of the total number of defects. And, row three indicates the cumulative % contribution for the categories. In Figure 28, Registration and Authorization account for 87.8% of the overall defects.

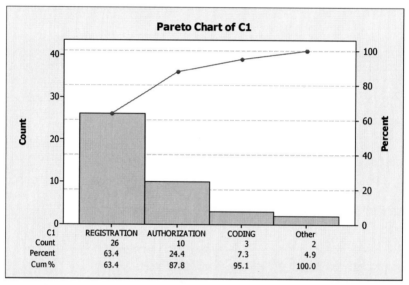

Figure 28

How do I do it?

Step 1: Identify the categories.

Step 2: Quantify the total of each category.

Step 3: Place the data in Minitab.
Use one column to list all the categories, and another to list their respective totals. See Figure 29.

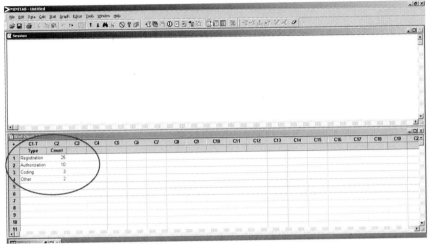

Figure 29

Step 4: Run the Pareto Chart.

Go to: Stat>Quality Tools>Pareto Chart. See Figure 29.

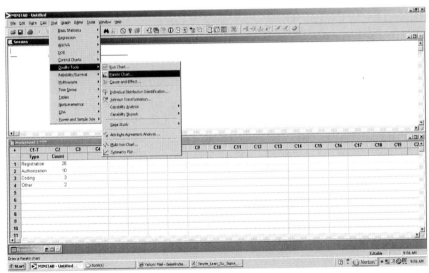

Figure 30

Select the "Chart defects table." See Figure 30.

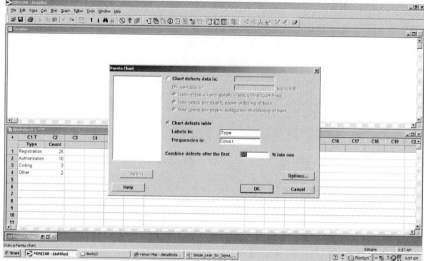

Figure 31

- Select the column with the categories into the "labels in" field.
- Select the column with the count into the "Frequencies in" field.
- Click "OK."
- You should see the chart in Figure 31.

Descriptive Statistics is used to provide basic description about the behavior of a given data set. The two main features are the data's Central Tendency and Variability. This will be explained in detail later in the book. But, in simple, the Central Tendency is measured in three ways:

- *Average/Mean* measures the sum of all the numbers and divides it by the total number in the data set.
- *Median* organizes the data in numerical order and captures the number in the middle of the data set.
- *Mode* represents the number with the most frequency in the data set.

The common measurements for variability are:
- *Range* is the difference between the highest and the lowest number in the data set.
- *Standard Deviation* is a standard measurement of what the average difference between the values in the data set.

Consider the following data set: {1, 3, 5, 6, 5, 8, 5}

Central Tendency
- Mean = $(1+3+5+6+5+8+5) \div 7 = 4.7143$
- Median = 5;
  - Sort the data in numerical order: {1, 3, 5, 5, 5, 6, 8}
  - Median is the number in the middle: 5
- Mode = 5; 5 is the number that occurs most frequently

Variability
- Range = 8 (height number) – 1 (lowest number) = 7
- Standard Deviation = 2.2147 (calculated using Minitab)

Let's generate the Descriptive Statistics using Minitab.

Step 1: Enter the data into Minitab.

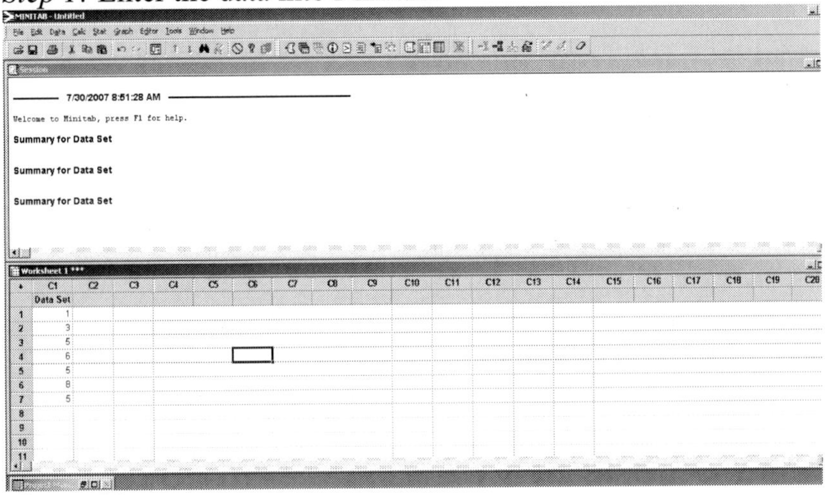

Figure 32

Step 2: Go to Stat>Basic Statistics>Graphical Summary.

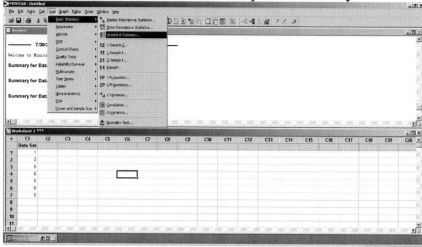

Figure 33

Step 3: Select the column with the data into the 'Variables' field and click 'OK.'

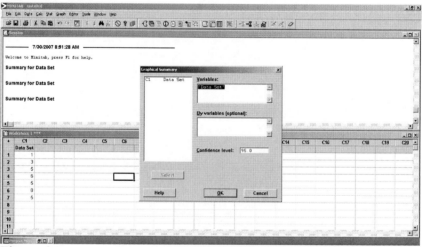

Figure 34

Step 4: Analyze the Descriptive Statistics.

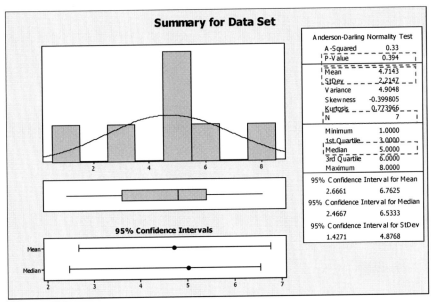

Figure 35

- The p-value is used to determine if the data is normally distributed. If p-value ≥ .05, then the data is normally distributed. The relevance for this is explained later in this book.
- You can gather the Mean, Standard Deviation and Median from the above graph.

Statistical Process Control (SPC) Charts display a given data set over time (in chronological order) and charts it relative to its control limits (boundaries) – this is done for both the average and the range. See below.

Step 1: Determine the SPC Chart to use based on the data type.

Data Type	Data Description	Possible SPCs
Discrete	% – (i.e Yes or no, compliant or non–compliant, correct or incorrect)	P–Chart
Discrete	Count	C–Chart
Continuous	Single values	I–MR
Continuous	Groups of 8 or less	X–Bar R
Continuous	Groups of 8 or more	X–Bar S

Table 12

Note that all SPC charts are in time series. (sort data values in chronological order—data value 1 comes before 2, and 2 before 3, and so forth)

Step 2: Generate the SPC Chart.

I-MR Chart

I-MR is an **I**ndividual **M**oving **R**ange chart. The SPC indicates two charts (as you will see below, both within the I-MR chart):

1. Data value
2. Range

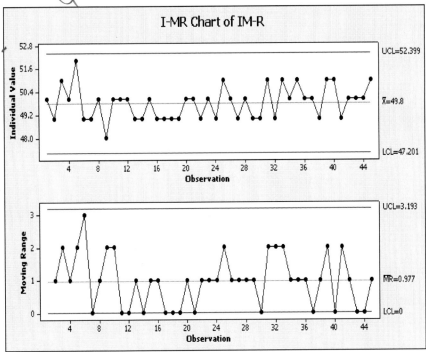

Figure 36

The top chart indicates the distribution of the data values, and the bottom chart indicates the distribution of the variation among the sequential data values. The top and bottom red lines represent the upper (UCL) and lower control limits (LCL). These lines indicate a distribution of 3 standard deviations. Points outside of these lines are out of the control boundaries and indicate a <u>special cause</u> of variation. Processes with special cause of variation are "out of control", as they are impacted by circumstances out of the control of the process. Additionally, the center line indicates the average variation. See Figure 36

As we can see, the average variation is 49.8 with a variation of 0.977. The system is stable and predictable and shows an average performance of 49.8, give or take 0.977.

Once again, we go to good old Minitab:
Stat > Control Charts > Variable Charts for individuals > I-MR:

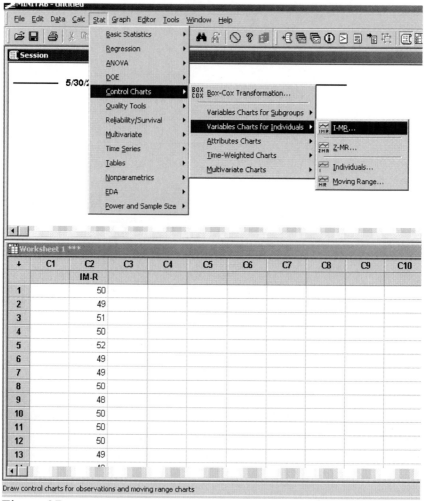

Figure 37

Enter the column with the data to be charted in the **Variable** field.

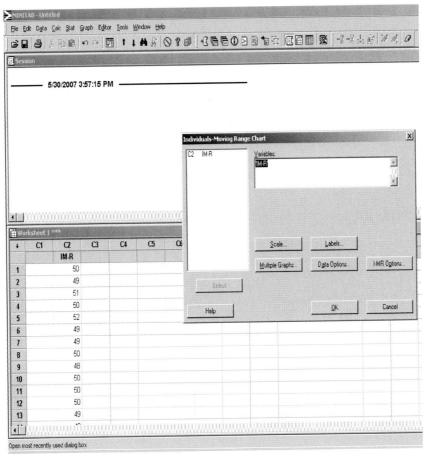

Figure 38

To graphically show the dates on the chart, select the **scale** button. Once you are in the scale form, select the **Stamp** radio button and choose the column with the dates into the **Stamp columns** field. This applies to all control charts.

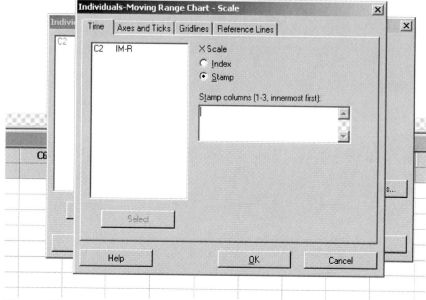

Figure 39

Xbar R Chart

Xbar R is a moving range chart that plots <u>the average of the</u> <u>subgroups</u> in the data range chart. Remember, the SPC indicates two charts: Data value and Range.

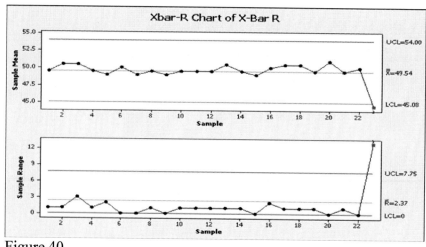

Figure 40

Simple Lean Six Sigma, Page 127 of 186

The top chart indicates the distribution of the average of the data values for the subgroups, and the bottom chart indicates the distribution of the variation among the sequential data values averages for the subgroups. As for other charts, the top and bottom red lines represent the upper (UCL) and lower control limits (LCL). These lines indicate a distribution of 3 standard deviations. Points outside of these lines are out of the control boundaries and indicate a special cause of variation. Processes with special cause of variation are "out of control", as they are impacted by circumstances out of the control of the process. Additionally, the center line indicates average variation.

The variation is calculated based on the range from data value to data value. The first data point in the top chart is the average of the first 3 numbers and the second data point is the average of the next three data points. The first data point in the moving range chart is the difference between data point 1 and data point 2.

See Figure 40. **The average variation is 49.54 with a variation of 2.37.** The system is not stable and predictable because point 23 is out of the bottom control limit for the top chart and out of the bottom limit for the bottom chart. **The average performance is 49.54, give or take 2.37.**

Generating an Xbar-R Chart:

Stat > Control Charts > Variable Charts for Subgroups > Xbar-R

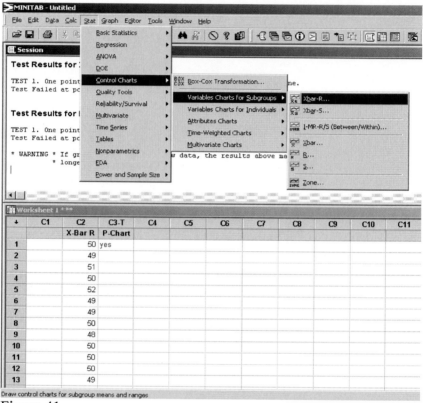

Figure 41

Enter the column with the data to be charted into the main field under the field stating "all observations for a chart are in one column." Now enter the subgroup size in the **subgroup size** field (Simple Note: make sure the values in the Minitab column selected are in chronological and in order by group as well!). Look at the following 4 data points:

Values	Group 1
Value 1	
Value 2	Average of value 1 and 2
Value 3	
Value 4	Average of value 3 and 4

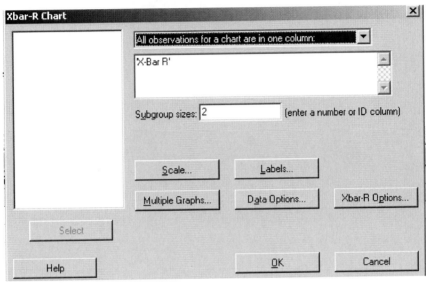

Figure 42

In the chart, the first data point constitutes of the average of values 1 and 2, and the second data point, the average of values 3 and 4.

Xbar S Chart

Xbar S is moving range chart that plots the average of the subgroups in the data standard deviation chart. As always, the SPC indicates two charts: Data value and Range.

The chart is identical to that of the Xbar-R. The only difference is the way the variation chart data points are calculated.

Generating an Xbar S Chart

Stat > Control Charts > Variable Charts for Subgroups> Xbar-S

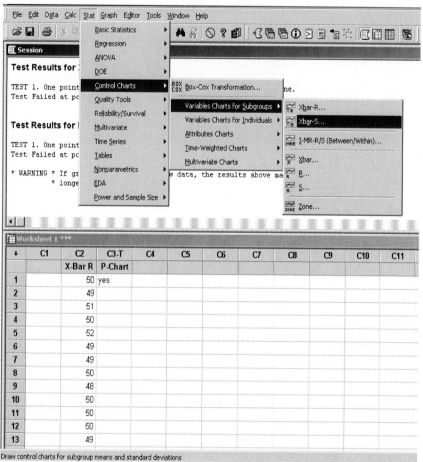

Figure 43

Enter the column with the data to be charted into the main field under the field stating "all observations for a chart are in one column." Now enter the subgroup size in the **subgroup size** field (Simple Note: make sure the values in the Minitab column selected are in chronological and in order by group as well!). Look at the following 4 data points:

Values	Group 1
Value 1	
Value 2	Average of value 1 and 2
Value 3	
Value 4	Average of value 3 and 4

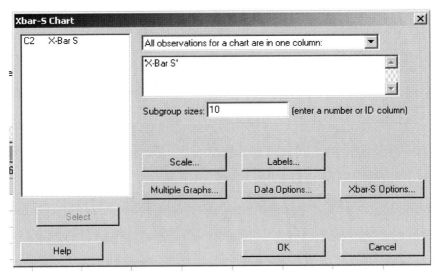

Figure 44

In this chart, the first data point constitutes of the average of values 1 and 2, and the second data point, the average of values 3 and 4.

P Chart

A "P Chart" measures the proportion distribution of the output under evaluation. This time, the SPC indicates only one chart: Data value.

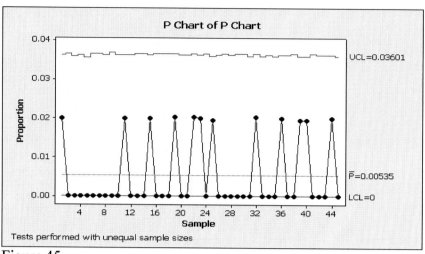

Figure 45

Generating a P Chart:

Stat > Control Charts > Attribute Charts > P Chart

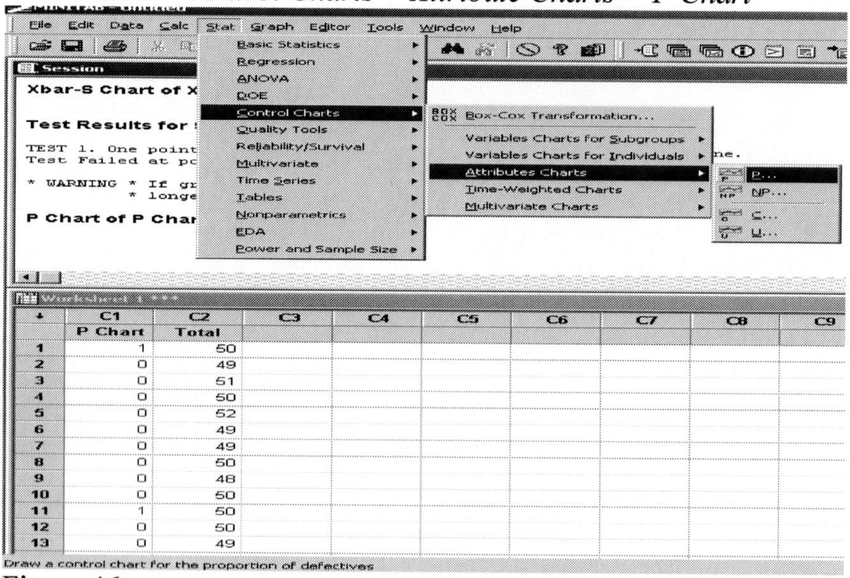

Figure 46

Enter the column with the data to be charted (numerator) in the
Variable field. Enter the subgroup size in the **subgroup sizes** field.
If the subgroup size is equal for all samples, simply type the
number.

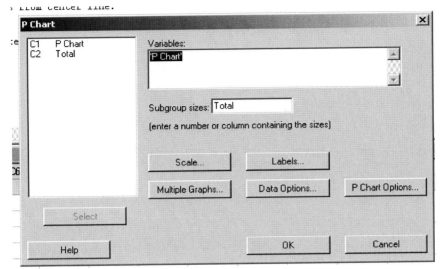

Figure 47

<u>P Chart Example</u>

A pen factory would like to know the percentage of pens from "Machine A" that are defective per day.

Each day is a data point. The numerator (which is data to be tracked and entered into the **variable** field) is the number of defective pens. The numerator and data entered in the **subgroup sizes** field is the total of number of pens produced by the machine per day.

C Chart

A "C Chart" measures the distribution of the output under evaluation for discrete count data. Also one chart only: Data value.

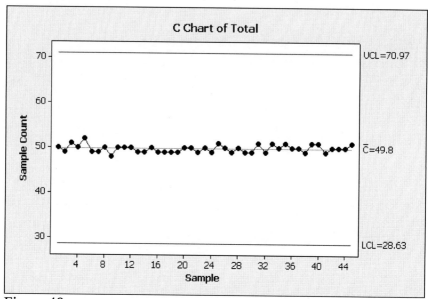

Figure 48

Generating a C Chart

Stat > Control Charts > Attribute Charts > C Chart

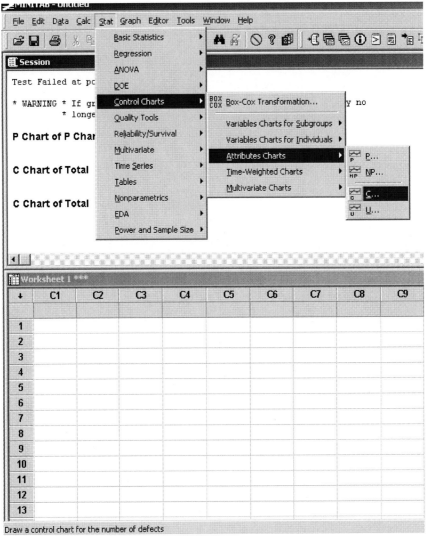

Figure 49

Enter the column with the data to be charted in the **Variable** field.

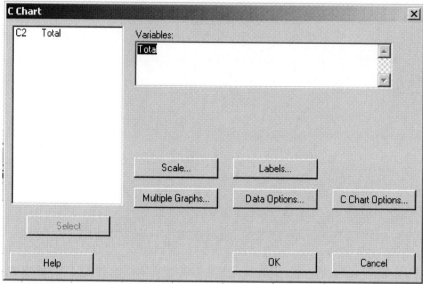

Figure 50

C Chart Example

A pen factory would like to know the number of pens from "Machine A" that are defective per day. Each day is a data point. The data to be tracked and entered into the **variable** field is the number of defective pens per day.

Step 6: Generate and interpret the respective SPC.

Before moving on to the Analyze phase, you should be able to precisely define what problems are occurring and define the underlying conditions that are likely to appear. You should have data in hand that you can use to demonstrate to your champion:
- What specifically is the main problem or problems (Baseline)?
- How did you prioritized and selected critical input, process and output measures (Detailed Process Mapping)?
- What have you done to validate the measurement system ?
- What patterns are exhibited in the data – What is the baseline (Shape, Center & Spread, Special Causes, Common Causes)?

- What the current process capability is (SPC & Spec Limits)

Chapter 4.6:

Phase 3, Analyze Phase

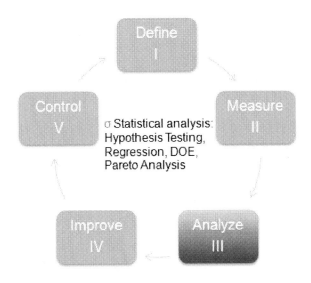

Cause-and-Effect Relationship

At the beginning of the Analyze phase we have a notion of the drivers impacting the CTQ, but we have not confirmed the cause-and-effect relationship by performing in-depth statistical analysis.

What is Statistical Significance?

Statistical Significance measures the probability of an event's occurrence. An event that is statistically significant is not due to chance or coincidence; therefore, if the relationship between the CTQ and the Xs is statistically significant then the observed behavior of the relationship has a high probability of continuing to occur. And, by altering the Xs, you can achieve the desired CTQ, or goal.

How do I do this?

The most challenging part of establishing statistical significance is identifying the appropriate statistical tool.

There are three possible tools that can be considered for normally distributed data:
- Hypothesis Testing
- Regression
- Design of Experiments ("DOE")

What does it mean to be normally distributed? Why is that important?

Normal distribution is part of a critical set of continuous probability distributions that are identified by two key parameters: average and variability. It is important because normally distributed data experiences a behavioral phenomenon known as the Central Limit Theory, which states that any set of independent and identically distributed, random variables will have a finite variance. And, if the variance is finite, it can be quantified (measured) and used to measure the level of consistency within any given process.

What is an average?

It is the tendency, or likely hood of a number. If you have a process that had the following outcomes: 4, 2, 4 and 2 then you can state that if the process where to occur ten more times, it is likely that the number would be about 3. This is calculated as follows:

Average = sum of the numbers / count of the numbers summed
       = (4+2+4+2)/4 = 3

What is variability?

It's what measures the difference between the numbers in a data set. Why is that important? Because if the numbers are far apart, then the average is not a good representation of what the process can produce. Take the following data sets:

Set 1: 1, 9

Set 2: 5, 5

The average to both data sets is 5, but data Set 1 is not really representative of any reliable pattern. This is because one number is 1 and the other is 9. So, you can't assume the outcome of the next occurrence would be around 5.

Set 1: average = (1+9)/2 = 5

Set 2: average = (5+5)/2 = 5

How do I know which statistical test to use?

The appropriate test depends on several factors:
- Data type
- Number of variables

- If the variables have a likely interaction (cause and effect relationship between the key Xs)
- If the data is paired: if the each part can be retested
- If the analysis is going to be based on the average of the data set, or the variation
- If data is linear or not

Begin by determining the data type.

Hypothesis testing is used to study discrete data, Regression is used to study continuous data and DOE is used to study either continuous or discrete data.

What is discrete and continuous data?

Discrete (Attribute) data is finite in count and cannot be subdivided into meaningful subcategories. If you cannot have a half of something, it is discrete. As an example, you cannot have a half of a person or half of a defect. Some examples include:
- Attribute (i.e. Y/N, Go/No Go, etc.)
- Binary (i.e. 0, 1)
- Categorical (i.e. Monday, Tuesday, Wednesday)
- Count (i.e. 1, 2, 3, 4, 5, etc.)

Continuous (measurement) data is infinite in count and can be meaningfully subdivided. If you can have a half of something, it is continuous. Some examples include:
- Height
- Weight
- Time

NOTE: **PROPORTION (%) IS DISCRETE DATA**, AS ITS NUMERATOR AND DENOMINATOR ARE BOTH DISCRETE!

There are different statistical tools within each of the mentioned categories. The available tools within each category are as follows:

- Hypothesis Testing:
    - *t*-test
    - Paired *t*-test
    - ANOVA (F-tests)
    - ANOVA (Homogeneity of Variance)
    - Chi-Squared Test
    - 2-Proportion Test
- Regression
    - Simple
    - Multi-linear
    - Curvi-linear
    - Logistic
- Design of Experiments ("DOE")
    - 2 Level Full Factorial
    - Fractional Factorial
    - General Model
    - Response Surface

Before we learn in depth when to use each of these tests, let's learn a little background on the different types of tests.

Hypothesis Testing is as, the name implies, is a *test* to establish if there is a statistically significant difference between groups. It is often used when the input variables (Xs) are discrete. The type of test depends on whether the output variable (CTQ) is continuous or discrete. In the event of a **continuous CTQ and discrete Xs**, the appropriate tests are:

- **T-test** is used when there is one X that measures no more than two groups of data. As an example, if you are determining if the processing time between two suppliers differs, you could use the t-test. The processing time (CTQ) is being compared among two types of suppliers (X): suppliers one and two.

- **Paired t-test** is just as the t-test, but assumes that the same product or transaction can be undone in order to redo it under the second type. As an example, you can use this methodology if you are trying to determine if two methodologies have similar outcomes. In this event, you would construct a product, and undo it in order to redo it using a different methodology.

- **ANOVA** is used in the same format and manner as the t-test, but with more than two groups to compare. As an example, suppose you are comparing three or four suppliers, you can use this tool to determine if there is a statistical difference between the processing times among the suppliers.

In the event where both the **CTQ and Xs are discrete**, the following tests are applicable:

- **Chi-Squared** is used as the ANOVA, but assuming that the CTQ is discrete.
- **2-Proportion Test** is used as the t-test, but when the CTQ is discrete.

For all of the above, the test is composed of two parts, the Null and Alternate hypothesis:

The Null hypothesis indicates the assumption being tested - that the groups are the same, while the alternate assumes the exact opposite of that which the null is testing. This is represented in the following format:

Ho: Groups are the same
Ha: Groups are not the same

There are two key errors that can be made with hypothesis testing:
1) Assume the groups are the same, when in reality they are different. This is known as an **Alpha error**.
2) Assume the groups are different, when in reality they are same. This is known as a **Beta error**.

The p-value (probability value) is used to determine whether to reject a hypothesis or not.

The probability of making an Alpha error is compared to the resulting probability from the statistical analysis (p-value). And if, the probability of an Alpha error (p-value) is greater than the tolerance of alpha (as predetermined), then the hypothesis is rejected. A standard alpha tolerance level is 5%, or .05.

That is, if the p-value < the set alpha, then the Null is rejected and the alternate is assumed.

Regression Analysis quantifies the relationship between the CTQ and the X(s) through a method known as the sum of least squares.

Much like in hypothesis testing, in regression you are also testing a hypothesis. But, in this case, it is not based on generalizations of 'like' and not 'alike.' It is a relationship that is quantified and expressed in the form of an equation:

$$Y = b_0 + b_1X_1$$

b_0 = **intercept** (where the line crosses X= 0)
b_1 = **slope** (rise over run, or change in Y per unit increase in X)

The slope of b_1 represents the magnitude of the relationship between the given X and Y. If b_1 is 1, then for every change in X_1 you have an equal change in Y (1 x anything = the same value. Now, if b_1 equals zero, then it does not matter what the value for X is, the relationship does not exist because any change in X will not drive a change in Y. This is because zero x anything is zero.

This equation represents the expected behavior and values for the relationship between the CTQ and the Xs. The equation is often referred to as a *model*.

Once the data is collected, it is plotted and the difference between the observed value and the expected values are calculated. These values are called residuals. They are just that: the residuals of the model to the actual values. See Figure 51. The straight line is the modeled relationship, and the dots (data points) are the actual data collected.

In order to rely on the regression analysis, the residuals must be independent and normally distributed.

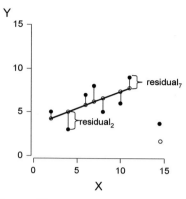

Figure 51

These values are then squared and summed in order to capture the variability in of the process that is explained or captured by the *model* (the assumed relationship). That number is called the **R-squared**.

The R-Squared is the % the variation in the process that is explained by the model (assumed relationship). If this number is high (i.e. 90%) That means that by improving or optimizing the quantified relationship, you can improve 90% of the variation.

If this number, however, is low (i.e. 10%), then it does not matter or make sense to optimize the relationship since at best you will be able to improve 10% of the variation.

This test is used when the Xs are continuous. The are four main types of regression analysis:

- Simple Linear Regression is used when there is only one critical X, and the relationship between the X and the CTQ is linear.
- What does it mean to have a linear relationship? Simply, that the Xs (independent variable) drive a proportionate impact on the CTQ (the variable that is dependent on the independent variable X).

- Multiple Linear Regression is the same as the simple linear regression, but is used when there is more than one X.
- Logistic Regression is used when the CTQ is discrete.
- Curvi-linear Regression is used when the relationship between the Xs and the CTQ follows a curvy pattern.

The first step to completing any regression analysis is to **PLOT THE DATA! This can be done through a scatter plot or a matrix plot.** You need to plot the data to properly determine the nature of the relationship between the X(s) and the CTQ, and be able to assign the appropriate regression. A scatter plot, or matrix plot, can be used to graphically display the relationship between the CTQ and the Xs:

- Scatter Plot visually displays the relationships among two variables.
- Matrix Plot visually displays the relationships among many variables.

Design of Experiments ("DOE") is a tool that effectively and efficiently analyses the cause-and-effect relationship between the Xs and the CTQ. Like with regression, the relationship between the factors (Xs) and the CTQ is quantified and represented in the form of an equation - the *model*. The underlying assumptions are the same.

In English?

Let's start by discussing the components within a DOE:

$$2^k_R$$

Figure 52

Figure 52 is the standard format for representing a DOE. These are the core components to a DOE:

- k is used to indicate the number of Factors in the experiment. You can think of factors as your Xs. And, you are going to use and manipulate the factors to determine the effect they, or their interaction, have on the response variable. The response variable is the dependent variable in the equation we explained in the measure phase. It is a dependent variable because it depends on the setting of the independent variables (Xs).
- 2 is the Level for the factors. This number can be different, but the most commonly used DOE is the two level factorial. The level represents the number of setting at which you are testing the respective factor. As an example, assume you are measuring the effect of caloric intake and body composition on weight. But you only care about the impact of high and low caloric intake on weight loss; and, there are three body compositions (Endo, Ecto and Mesomorph). Then you have two factors and the factors have two and three levels, respectively.

- R indicates the desired level of Resolution for the experiment. The resolution depends on the predetermined level of Confounding built into the experiment. What does that mean?

Assume you have a CTQ and three Xs. The equation we discussed earlier in the measure phase would indicate: CTQ = X1 + X2 +X3. In this case the CTQ is the response, or the dependent variable on X1, X2, and X3. It is dependent because the levels or setting of the Xs drive the value of the CTQ.

In the world of DOE, each of the Xs is a main effect (Factor). That is, a main variable whose effect on the response variable (CTQ) will be measured. But, DOE also quantifies the effect of a cause-and-effect relationship of the Xs on the CTQ. The cause-and-effect relationship is called the *interaction* between the factors (Xs).

So, the total number of variables that will be analyzed will be seven:

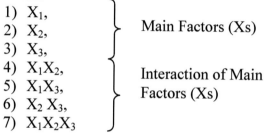

1) X_1,
2) X_2,   Main Factors (Xs)
3) X_3,
4) X_1X_2,
5) X_1X_3,   Interaction of Main
6) $X_2 X_3$,   Factors (Xs)
7) $X_1X_2X_3$

With seven variables to measure, the number of data points to collect is large. You may choose to confound some of the variables in order to reduce the number of data points to collect. Confounding is measuring the effect of multiple variables as one. In the above example, if you chose to confound main effects and three-way interactions, instead of being able to see the effect that X_1 has on the CTQ, you would see the effect that $X_1 + X_1X_2X_3$ have on the CTQ. This is only reasonable if you know that the probability of the three-way interaction having a high effect or equivalent effect than the main effect is low. This is one of the reasons that high process knowledge is important in conducting a DOE.

Assume that the effect on the CTQ was 10. There is more than one way to get the sum of ten out of two numbers. Two possible ways are 1+9 and 5+5. If you know that the probability of $X_1X_2X_3$ having an effect on the CTQ is low, you can confound the two because you know the majority of the quantified effect is relevant to X_1.

Following is a table of the most common resolutions and the relative confounding of factors:

Resolution	Confounding
III	Main Effect are confounded with two way interactions.
IV	Main Effects are confounded with Three Way interactions; and, Two Way interactions are confounded other Two Way interactions.
V	Main Effects are confounded with Four Way interactions; and, Two Way interactions are confounded with Three Way interactions.
Full Factorial	There is no confounding.

Table 13

Now what? Determine the number of data points to collect and make adjustments as needed in order to design the appropriate DOE.

The number of data points to be collected is calculated using the following basic components: number of factors, number of levels within each factor, resolution, repetition, and repeatability. We learned what the number of factors, levels, and resolution are, but what about repetition and repeatability?

Let's begin with the ones we have learned. The core number of data points is a set of combinations determined by the number of factors and levels within each factor.

If we take the previously mentioned weight loss example, weight loss is the response variable (CTQ/Dependent Variable). The independent variables (Xs) are calories and body constitution. In this event, the response variable is continuous; and one of the Xs is continuous (caloric intake). But only the impact of high and low is important. So, the effect will be tested on two levels: 1,000 calories and 5,000 calories. Body type, however, consists of three different types. And, there for has three levels.

If we address the main purpose of a DOE, all possible combinations of the given factors and levels within the factors need to be measured in order to quantify the cause-and-effect relationship. The core set of combinations and data points is equal to the multiplication of the total number of levels for each factor:

2 (High and Low setting for caloric intake) x 3 (Types of body composition) = 6,

1) 1,000 Calories; Endomorph
2) 5,000 Calories; Endomorph
3) 1,000 Calories; Ectomorph
4) 5,000 Calories; Ectomorph
5) 1,000 Calories; Mesomorph
6) 5,000 Calories; Mesomorph

The above are the core combinations for the response under study. That is, there is only one data point for each type of combination of settings within the factors. In order to have multiple data points of each type of combination, each combination needs to be run more multiple times within one experiment. The multiple runs of combinations within an experiment is known as **repeats**

A *replicate* is the number of times you run the entire experiment. Using the above example, if you wanted to run the experiment four times then your total number of runs would equal [2 (High and Low setting for caloric intake) x 3 (Types of body composition)] x 4 = 24,
. Now, as the number of factors, repeats and replicates increase, the number of combinations grows exponentially.
In the above example you saw a mixture of levels between the factors and within one experiment. This is not the most common scenario. The most common scenario is to have all factors have an equal number of levels for each factor.

Using the above example, if you only want to measure the impact with respect to two body types: Endomorph and Mesomorph. Then, you have two levels for each of the factors (high, low; endo, meso). With only one repeat and only one run, the total number of combinations or runs $= 2^2 = 2x2 = 4$.

DOE Basics

- DOE is conducted with live data through an experiment setting and data collection gathering plan. HISTORICAL DATA CANNOT BE USED TO RUN A DESIGN OF EXPERIMENT!

- Data is collected in a random manner as the data plan generated by the DOE design is random. This helps to eliminate the impact of factors that are out of your control and you sometimes don't even know they exist. These are called *lurking variables*.

- Helps to provide in sight on the process by proving the direct effect of the variables on the CTQ as well as quantify the interaction between the variables.

DO NOT CONDUCT A DOE IF THE PROCESS IS NOT CAPABLE OF CONTROLLING THE SETTINGS ISSUED BY THE DESIGN, THERE IS NO KNOWLEDGE OF THE Xs THAT IMPACT THE CTQ, OR THE PROCESS IS NOT IN STATISTICAL CONTROL!

Note: You established statistical control for the process in the measure phase through the SPC analysis.

DOE Guideline Questions

1. Is management willing to commit the needed resources?

2. Are process requirements clearly defined?
3. How much is known about the process?
    - Variation, centering, defect levels.
    - The source of variation.
    - Measurement systems.
4. What is the goal of project?
    - Identify critical parameters.
    - Determine sources of variation.
    - Center processes.
    - Reduce variation.
    - Design more robust processes.
5. What are the response variables?
6. How is the response variables measured?
7. Can we meet our goals through a DOE?
8. What is the risk in conducting the DOE? What is the risk in not conducting the DOE?

Answering these questions can help you determine if a DOE is appropriate - at this time.

Step 1: Define Goals and Objectives. This as completed in the define phase through the Project Charter, SIPOC and VOC.

Step 2: Determine what is known in qualitative and quantitative Terms. This was established in the measure phase by the operational definition and SPC analysis.

Step 3: Select factors. This was identified in the measure phase as the Xs.

Step 4: Determine at which levels of the factors it is important to evaluate the effect on the response variable. In the weight loss example, caloric intake is a continuous X, but only the impact of the low and high caloric intake is relevant with respect to weight loss. So, instead of measuring your daily weight with respect to your caloric intake, you would be preset to each a predetermined amount of caloric intake and then tract the weight with respect to the high and low levels of caloric intake.

Step 5: Choose and Set Up the Appropriate Experimental Design

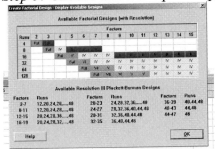

Figure 53

You can view the resolution and number of runs based on the number of factors. Also, determine if the relationship between the Xs and the CTQ are linear. If the relationship is not linear, you may want to consider running a response surface. See details in Appendix B.

Step 5: Run the Experiment and Evaluate/Interpret the results. See **Appendix B** for a detailed step-by-step on conducting and evaluating a DOE.

Step 6: Define Next Steps. Determine if there is any noise (variation) that needs to be controlled or if different or additional levels are needed within the factors.

Please refer to **Appendix B** for a detailed walk through on how to complete any of the tools mentioned within the statistical analysis section of this book.

Chapter 4.7:

Phase 4, Improve Phase

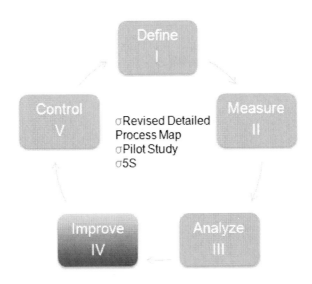

Revised Process

Use the value and statistical analysis from the analyze phase, and determine a new structure that best streamlines the process by eliminating unnecessary functions. All stakeholders should be readily involved in the new design for optimal structure as well as possess a sense of involvement and pride that will facilitate the ability to implement solution.

Creating the Revised Process Map

Once the value analysis has been completed, visually show the major process change(s). That is, the proposal to eliminate all Non-Required-Non-Value-Added steps from the process. Please follow the following format for graphically displaying the process steps' value base:

- *Value-Added* and *Required-Non-Value Added* – Leave as is
- *Non-Required-Non-Value Added* – Cross out by placing a big 'X' over the shape representing the process step

Using the previously described example, visually display the rough changes:

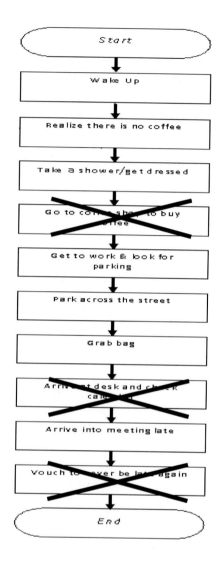

Figure 54

Based on Figure 54, three out of ten process steps can be eliminated from the process. Along with this change, the Non-Required-Non-Value-Added steps will be analyzed for optimization of the flow, and the overall structure will be analyzed to find the optimal flow for the respective process.

Now what?

Now, let's map the proposed process taking into account that the objective is <u>to improve</u> the way Value-Added steps <u>are performed</u> and reduce the number of (as well as waste within) the Required-Value-Added steps.

The following questions can be used to help achieve the objective within each of the value classifications:

Value-Added
- How can this be better?
- How do other places do it?
- Is there a national or global benchmark?
- Assuming there are no restrictions, how should the process function?
- What is the best way the process can be accomplished?
- Did the customers say anything about this? If so, what?
- What is required?

Required-Value-Added

- How can this be reduced to the minimum amount required?
- Is there a way to make the process more efficient?
- What do other places do?
- Are there any benchmarks?
- What is required?
- Did the customer's say anything about this? If so, what?

Use the above set of questions along with the suggestions made within the voice of the customer and design the optimal flow. Let's reason through the previous example step by step:
1) What is the optimal time to wake up?

2) How do other people get to work?

3) How long is the drive?

4) How can I make sure that I don't wake up to realize there is no coffee? If coffee is a must for me, how can I reduce the amount of times I have to rework my schedule to have a cup?

5) How do I make sure I make it to my morning meetings on time without going to the office to check my schedule the morning of the meeting?

Here is a sample of a revised flow for the previous example:

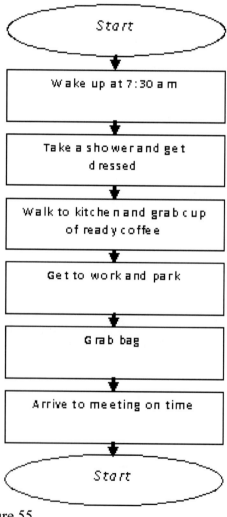

Figure 55

Next, analyze the proposed flow to ensure it follows the fundamentals of an improved process: 5S concept.

Once all the recommendations have been approved, a pilot study **MUST** be conducted prior to implementing any solutions as illustrated in the revised flow.

What is a Pilot?

A pilot is a test of a proposed solution and it can also test the implementation.

It consists of following properties and has the following characteristics:

- Implementation of the proposed solution, performed on a small scale
- Used to evaluate both the solution and the implementation
- It serves to validate the recommendations and provides insight on minor or major improvements that need to be made prior to going into production
- Gives data about expected results and exposes issues in the implementation plan
- Learn about and refine solution
- Understand risks
- Demonstrate expected results
- Smooth implementation
- Facilitate buy-in
- Identify previously unknown performance problems.

Pilot Planning Checklist
\

- Set a timeline and plans
  - o Detailed list of action items and the respective deadlines.
  - o Start and stop dates for pilot.

- - Action plan for problems that arise.
  - Establish budget & resource constraints
  - Define new procedures and written instructions for the pilot, and supported by visual aids, flowcharts, any other materials
- Prepare stakeholders.
- Pilot participants understand roles and responsibilities
- New documentation and procedures reviewed and explained to all pilot participants
- People affected by the change are informed of its scope and timing
- Define how to measure success/failure and capture lessons
- Data collection / monitoring plan for both methods and results

Evaluate the Pilot

- Compare results against the original definition of a defect and against CTQs.
- Verify that there is an improvement.
- Recalculate process sigma and process capability.
- Analyze causal relationships and process conditions.
- Compare the data from before the pilot to that of the data after the pilot and you should see an improvement on the SPC.

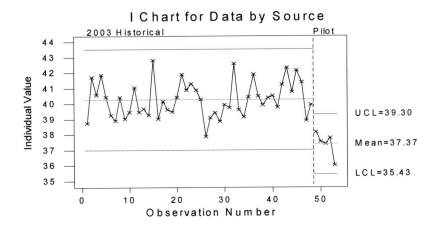

Figure 56

How do I create a before and after I-MR chart?

Organize the data from before the pilot in chronological order and create a second column next to it called "before." Then organize the data from the pilot in chronological order and place the "after" data. Once you are in the form for the respective control chart, select **chart options** and then within options select the **stages** tab. Enter the column with the before and after category. Click OK; you should see a chart like the one in Figure 56.

Pilot... then implement

Analyze the results of the pilot(s) to determine if you have reached a solution that achieves your performance goals. If you did, proceed with implementation. If not, revisit suggested restructure.

Chapter 4.8:

Phase 5, Control Phase

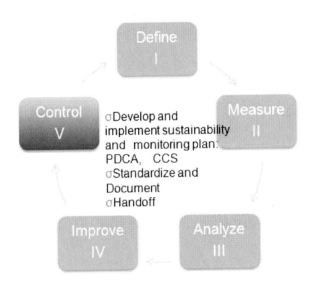

Once the project has been successfully piloted and implementation underway, outcomes sustainability begins. A proper monitoring plan needs to be set such that monitoring factors are built in to the process.

A common monitoring tool is the Plan/Do Check Act (Figure 57):

Plan/do – reflects the new process map with the detail for easy interpretation of the process.

Check/Study – is the built-in mechanism to track and analyze the data and its compliance in order to prevent it from reverting to previous conditions.

Act – reflects the corrective actions when the new flow is violated. If these actions are not maintained with reinforcement from the appropriate <u>management</u> person or people, this is a factor that is able to disappear.

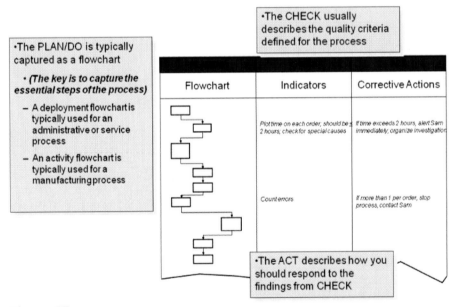

Figure 57

For optimal sustainability, this tool needs to be tied into an organizational or departmental dashboard or report.

FMEA

Complete the FMEA introduced in the measurement phase to include a detailed action taken to improve the given variables. Rescore the severity, occurrence and detection in order to generate and track the RPN within the FMEA. In the event that a failure occurs you can reach the problem in a relatively simple manner. See Figure 58.

Critical Parameter	Potential Failure Mode	Potential Effect of Failure(s)	S E V	Cause(s)	O C C U R	Current Process Controls	D E T	R P N	Recommended Actions	Responsibility & Target Date	Action Results			
											Actions Taken	S E V	O C C	D E T	R P N
X₁ (Cause 1)														
X₂ (Cause 2)														

Figure 58

Once the sustainability plan and FMEA are complete, the process needs to be properly standardized across all areas and units <u>with documentation of the approach</u>; finally, handoff the entire documentation and detailed instructions to the process owner.

Chapter 5:

Concluding Remarks

In conclusion, the world of P²I is comprehensive and has numerous reliable approaches. They key to success is management infrastructure in leadership, communication and teamwork.

Here are some common problems when driving structured organizational excellence:

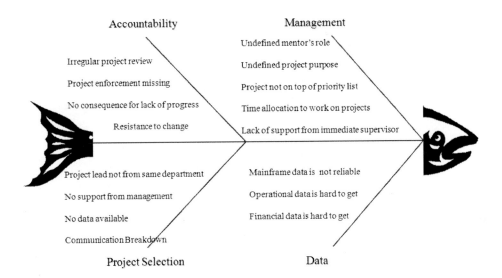

Take-Away

- Problem Solving and Process Improvements are complex business essentials.
- The key component to macro and micro problem solving is communication, leadership and teamwork. Being a good team player is critical.
- Lean Six Sigma embeds the core engineering problem solving skills and culture into all areas of expertise such that it becomes a way of life for all.
- Lean aims to reduce unnecessary steps and/or functions.
- Six Sigma is a state of performance that drives 3.4 defects for every million opportunities.
- Six Sigma is a known and tested methodology (DMAIC) that achieves a Six Sigma State of performance through the use of rigorous data analysis and statistical tools as well as

key tools that support the conversion of soft (qualitative) goals into hard (quantitative) goals.

- You need to know where you are to understand where you are going! And, the journey is critical to ensure successful arrival to the final destination!

D-M-A-I-C Summary

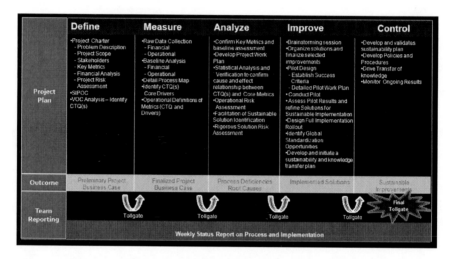

	Define	Measure	Analyze	Improve	Control
Project Plan	•Project Charter - Problem Description - Project Scope - Stakeholders - Key Metrics - Financial Analysis - Project Risk Assessment •SIPOC •VOC Analysis – Identify CTQ(s)	•Raw Data Collection - Financial - Operational •Baseline Analysis - Financial - Operational •Detail Process Map •Identify CTQ(s) Core Drivers •Operational Definitions of Metrics (CTQ and Drivers)	•Confirm Key Metrics and baseline assessment •Develop Project Work Plan •Statistical Analysis and Verification to confirm cause and effect relationship between CTQ(s) and Core Metrics •Operational Risk Assessment •Facilitation of Sustainable Solution Identification •Rigorous Solution Risk Assessment	•Brainstorming session •Organize solutions and finalize selected improvements •Pilot Design - Establish Success Criteria - Detailed Pilot Work Plan •Conduct Pilot •Assess Pilot Results and refine Solutions for Sustainable Implementation •Design Full Implementation Rollout •Identify Global Standardization Opportunities •Develop and initiate a sustainability and knowledge transfer plan	•Develop and validates sustainability plan •Develop Policies and Procedures •Drive Transfer of knowledge •Monitor Ongoing Results
Outcome	Preliminary Project Business Case	Finalized Project Business Case	Process Deficiencies Root Causes	Implemented Solutions	Sustainable Improvements
Team Reporting	Tollgate	Tollgate	Tollgate	Tollgate	Final Tollgate
	Weekly Status Report on Process and Implementation				

We hope this book has been helpful in teaching you the *why* and *how* of advanced P^{2}I using Lean Six Sigma.

This book is part of a ***Simple*** Book series:

Simple CCS vs. Dashboard

Explains the challenges of communication within organizations, and discusses how to systematically structure and align goals throughout organizations in order to improve management and effectively drive continuous improvement.

Simple Process Improvement (P^{2}I)

Lean, Six Sigma and Lean Six Sigma are advanced process improvement tools driven by statistics and/or engineering calculations/logistics. As such, it may be difficult to fit it into varying levels of education and background.

If you are interested in a simpler, and effective, process improvement framework, please feel free to read the *Simple Process Improvement (P²I)* book.

Have fun driving change!

If you are interested in pursuing certification in any of the discussed methods, please contact us:

DEIVIN
PO BOX 560728
Miami, FL 33256
Office: 305.663.3432
Email: info@deivin.com
www.deivin.com

Appendix A: Process Sigma Table

Process Sigma	Defects Per Million Opportunities (DPMO)	Process Sigma	Defects Per Million Opportunities (DPMO)
6.00	3.4	3.40	28,700
5.92	5	3.30	35,900
5.81	8	3.20	44,600
5.76	10	3.10	54,800
5.61	20	3.00	66,800
5.51	30	2.90	80,800
5.44	40	2.80	96,800
5.31	70	2.70	115,000
5.22	100	2.60	135,000
5.12	150	2.50	158,000
5.00	230	2.40	184,000
4.91	330	2.30	212,000
4.80	480	2.20	242,000
4.70	680	2.10	274,000
4.60	960	2.00	308,000
4.50	1,350	1.90	344,000
4.40	1,860	1.80	382,000
4.30	2,550	1.70	420,000
4.20	3,460	1.60	460,000
4.10	4,660	1.50	500,000
4.00	6,210	1.40	540,000
3.90	8,190	1.32	570,000
3.80	10,700	1.22	610,000
3.70	13,900	1.11	650,000
3.60	17,800	≤1.00	≥690,000
3.50	22,700		